D0969018

WHAT OTHER PEOPLE ARE SAYING ABOUT *FINDING THE SOUL OF BIG BUSINESS*

"The dominant philosophy of American business today is to make money without regard to integrity and moral values. Ego and greed have become the pillars of "success." Business has lost its way and our economy is suffering because of it. Congratulations to Paula Marshall for not only believing that business can have a soul, but putting her beliefs into actions. She leads our organization with an everlasting commitment to putting humanity before profits. I am privileged to have worked with her for almost two decades and have been a witness to what a company with a soul can accomplish. This book describes how Paula has achieved success by leading with her heart."

Bill Chew
CFO
The Bama companies, Inc.
Formerly with Pricewaterhouse Coopers

"Paula Marshall is an extraordinary leader who challenges conventional management practices with a unique blend of emotional intelligence and uncanny intuition. Paula's leadership encourages everyone to bring their full and true self to work each day and shed the corporate armor. If you have ever said to yourself, "There has got to be a better way to work," then you'll enjoy Paula's perspective on running a company in today's challenging global economy."

Mark J. Bendix
COO
The Bama Companies, Inc.
Former Sr. Executive Vice President
General Mills Foodservice Division

"Read *Finding the Soul of Big Business* to see what's possible when a CEO simultaneously leads with heart AND mind. In today's troubling economy, it's no longer business as usual. What Paula offers is a practical, personal and deeply integrated way of leading any organization. What impressed me most is how simple the solution is, if we could just open up and let go. At times, when reading it, I thought I was reading Zen and the Art of Manufacturing Dough!"

Cristi Dingle
Marketing Research
The Bama Companies, Inc.

FINDING THE
SOUL OF
BIG BUSINESS

ONE COMPANY'S EGO ELIMINATION STRATEGY

PAULA MARSHALL

The Soul of Big Business:
One Company's Ego Elimination Strategy
ISBN: 0-88144-326-3
Copyright © 2009 by Paula Marshall

Published by
YORKSHIRE PUBLISHING
9731 East 54th Street
Tulsa, Oklahoma 74146
www.yorkshirepublishing.com

Printed in Canada

Published in the United States of America. All rights reserved under International Copyright Law. No portion of this book may be used or reproduced by any means, graphic, electronic or mechanical including photocopying, recording, taping or by any information storage retrieval system without the express written permission of the author, except in the case of brief quotations embodied in critical articles and reviews.

TABLE OF CONTENTS

INTRODUCTION

Too often businesses, large and small, have structured themselves to be goal oriented. Milestones, statistics and the bottom line are pursued like quarry—pelts to be displayed on the belts of CEOs.

Business leaders cannot be faulted for such approaches because, for the most part, we all are products of a post-twentieth century Western (American) culture that sees society in terms of winners and losers. Worth is too often ascribed to birth order, gender, race, region, class and any other characteristics that can be assigned a category.

As a product of this culture, for years I put on a "happy face" and denied the feelings and instincts that are more than what is labeled as "woman's intuition." Over the years I began to trust that inner voice, which at times was so quiet I had to strain to hear it, or was so loud I wished there was a volume control to silence it. It is from this voice that I came to understand that each aspect of our lives, from learning to ride a bicycle to graduating from college, from parenting a child to running a business, is not about crossing an imaginary goal line or speeding towards a checkered flag; it is about the journey we take collectively and individually.

Journey is about integrity and stamina and risk and choice. Journey is a continuous process where every hour of every day you are putting one foot in front of the other, moving forward. Journey is intention.

Intention is your personal mission statement. More than a wish list or a bucket list, your intention is choice based, moving you from agony and despair to freedom and joy, from drudgery to accomplishment. Each step is taken with purpose towards what is possible rather than as a reaction to threat and fear.

Becoming CEO of Bama Companies, Inc. in 1985 was a shock and created a lot of fear for me personally. However, one of my greatest blessings from this role has been the opportunity to become friends with many of my coworkers. At our organization, we seek to know who you are and not give you a number. Numbers are not people! Because my parents before me always befriended their customers and their teammates, Bama has always been a "family" to me. I have had the privilege of working with some of the world's finest people. This experience has allowed me to recognize that none of us travel alone. Others are around to accompany us on our journey, and what we learn from our fellow travelers helps shape our intentions.

Those fellow travelers are our "life tutors"; they help us learn and grow. They are not fair weather friends, but are truly with us for the good times and the bad. Each one offers up messages, gifts and lessons at different times and at different places along the way. I have discovered that their teachings are always a perfect lesson to what I am experiencing at any given moment. Every person in our lives is put there for a reason, and I have learned from others throughout my life that nothing happens by accident.

Each person, place and thing in my life has helped me become the person I am today. I am a CEO, a mom, a friend, a daughter, a sister and a confidant. In every situation, my friends challenge my thinking. Some of them use stories, some use history, some use experiences and some teach me through their quick wit and teasing ways.

This book is an amalgamation of every lesson and every distinction I have learned and have applied to my intention as a CEO. I recognize that each employee, vendor and customer has embarked on their own journeys and our collective steps become the journey of Bama Companies, Inc.

Intention is only one aspect of putting a business on the path to excellence. Motivation is another criteria. As the CEO of Bama, it is my responsibility to inspire, empower and encourage my team and help them to discover their limitless creativity and potential to discover better ways to serve not only our suppliers and customers, but themselves as well.

To define my own intention and underlying motivation, I turned to the advice of Stephen R. Covey's book, *First Things First*. He explains why it is so important for each of us to write our own Personal Mission Statement. Writing a Personal Mission Statement, I found, is a very revealing exercise, but developing it allowed me to move from being a passive observer to an active participant. And as I refined and defined it, I found my voice. Covey says, "Voice is a unique personal significance—significance that is revealed as we face our greatest challenges and that make us equal to them."[1]

Finding my voice and defining my Personal Mission Statement has allowed me as a business leader to encourage others to find their voice, intention and motivation. I do this by putting my own ego aside, which allows me to empower others to bring out the best of himself or herself. Instead of motivating with fear, anxiety or reprisal (i.e., threat of losing a job or not getting a raise), at Bama we motivate with optimism.

Martin Seligman in his noted work, *Learned Optimism,* explained that "a person's belief about his or her setbacks are the main determinant as to whether the person remains motivated to go forward or gives up."[2] How much creative potential an individual uses is in direct proportion to how hopeful or discouraged he or she feels. People function at a lower range of potential when they are met with anxiety, fear, passive-aggressiveness, uncooperativeness and pessimism. These feelings are real and impact motivation.

---

[1] Dr. Stephen R. Covey. *The Eighth Habit: From Effectiveness to Greatness.* Free Press, New York, 2004, 5.

[2] Martin Seligman. *Learned Optimism: How to Change Your Mind and Your Life,* Simon and Schuster, Inc., New York, 1990, #.

God gave us feelings for a reason. Feelings allow us to grow, to understand our pain, to forgive, to love and have compassion for one another. Feelings left unconnected short-circuit the brain, the heart and the entire body leaving people numb. The "feel-less" human being is in an unhealthy condition.

Business leaders motivate by creating environments and encouraging conditions for their employees, suppliers and customers to exemplify more of their vast untapped human potential. The role of leaders is to appeal to the highest intention of people and to motivate them by allowing them to realize they are involved contributors whose participation matters. The business leader is not ego-driven; rather, he or she is driven by the ability to motivate others because they realize that success is dependent upon the performance of all associated with their enterprise.

The success of any business enterprise is dependent on the business leader's understanding, definition and reinforcement of the company's culture. As stated earlier, culture leaves a lasting mark on the participants of the culture. A business leader can shape a company's culture by modeling and articulating the desired culture. A culture is defined by the common, underlying values that all participants uphold as it conducts business. A shared culture can be a source of pride as an awareness of common values shows how the culture fosters opportunity for all of its participants. For example, everyone at Bama shares the value of exceeding customer expectation, a value that is clearly perceived and appreciated by our customers. Culture flows through vision. Vision illuminates the path of our shared journey and culture maps the way.

Leaders are manifested many ways: CEO, president, vice president, manager, coach, parent, teacher or even shepherd. What determines if a person is in actuality a leader is their ability to provide vision, motivation and support to the diverse members of their culture. A leader provides opportunities for participants to excel through encouragement rather than discouragement in a culture that values more than just financial gains. At Bama we know that heart, energy and spirit need to be nurtured. We strive to fulfill the psychological, social, professional and inspirational needs of our people.

Fostering this culture has been made possible at Bama thanks to the teachers and spiritual leaders who have shared their visions and expertise with me. I spent five years learning directly from Dr. Deming; I went to his seminars, took courses and became a sponge for his theories. I promised him that one day I would write a book and share my learnings. Dr. Deming had such an enormous impact on me in such a short time period, but it took me a long time to truly understand his theories.

His philosophies form the baseline of my management theories. More than anyone else, Dr. Deming provides a set of obligations for management to inquire about. They are not hard and fast rules, but obligations. He called them theories or "obligations of management."[3]

He truly believed in helping workers in all echelons of an organization. He became frustrated with traditional American business models. He hated rating and ranking people, and he hated robbing people of their pride. He understood how damaging those incentives are to the human psyche. He understood that a person with an open heart and mind could gain "profound knowledge" and become a "Spirit-filled leader."

One of my purposes in writing this book is to bring together Dr. Deming's teachings with some of my own personal philosophies for the purpose of changing "business as usual" in America and globally.

Besides Dr. Deming, I draw on the expertise of Dr. Stephen Covey, Peter Drucker, Carolyn Myss, Dusty Staub, Lawrence Hrebiniak, Scott McNealy, Thomas Nolan, Lloyd Provost, various business leaders and websites, recent newspaper articles, ancient myths and sacred writings. I draw wisdom and inspiration from the religions and mystics of the world. I draw wisdom from my children, my mom and my teammates. Knowledge truly is power for the Spirit-filled leader.

Bama Companies, Inc. hopes to be a representation of how business can be conducted in America and the world for the

---

[3] Dr. William Deming. *The New Economics for Industry, Government, Education,* Second edition, MIT Press, 121.

betterment of workers, suppliers, customers and consumers. That is my intention, and everyone who knows me knows that when I set my intention on something ... it happens ... join me on the journey.

CHAPTER ONE
PROFOUND KNOWLEDGE

Recent events of the twenty-first century are proof enough that business in America and throughout Western culture cannot continue their top-down archaic operations. The corporate culture of fast-tracked MBAs, CEO bonuses and winner-take-all has literally bankrupted our economy. Too often in corporations, businesses and even nonprofit organizations, people abandon their compassion and humanity when they walk through the office door. Companies and organizations can change and be prosperous again, but only with a sincere commitment to change business as usual.

I believe change starts with me. As the top officer of our business, the Bama Companies, I cannot ask something of someone else unless I am ready to do it myself. That is an important adage that is real at Bama. I believe executives spend too much time in companies telling others what to do, while not being willing to experience the process themselves.

No one can be ordered to change. Change requires a burning desire inside of a person's soul to change their behavior. They must assess the risks and determine for themselves if the pain of not doing something is worse than doing it.

Real change cannot be sustained out of fear. Most businesses and organizations use fear and intimidation to force immediate action, but as we have learned this only works in the short run. Lasting, meaningful change comes slowly from within each individual. Change must begin with a sincere effort inside yourself to believe YOU personally are in need of change. The change must be communicated consistently over and over again as patient, deliberate steps are taken over time to build and sustain a worthwhile operation.

The behaviors that drive these kinds of changes don't happen overnight. It takes a swell of activity, more often than not, started by one or two individuals with courage and stamina, and it takes years to mobilize others to the cause.

Change will come in a firestorm when people are ready ... it just takes the right message and the right timing coming together at the same time.

My primary business mentor (in addition to my parents) was Dr. W. Edward Deming. I spent five years learning directly from Dr. Deming; I went to his seminars, took courses and became a sponge for his theories. His philosophies form the baseline of my management theories. More than anyone else, Dr. Deming provides a set of guidelines for management. They are not hard and fast rules, but what he referred to as "obligations of management."

His theories were borne out of his frustration with how management operated and treated employees. He hated rating and ranking people, and he hated robbing people of their pride. He understood how damaging the "incentives" being used were to the human psyche. From Dr. Deming I learned that a person with an open heart and mind is able to gain what he called "profound knowledge" and become a "Spirit-filled leader."

Dr. Deming never called his theories spiritual, but I believe they are just that. In practicing his theories, leadership becomes spiritually awakened. His principles force our egos to retreat. The result allows us to listen, respect and offer compassion and forgiveness to others as we learn and implement new approaches for business operations.

Before a CEO or manager can implement or change the structure or practices of his or her company, they must take a step back and view their operations and organizations objectively from the outside. However, a view of their organizations is insufficient if business leaders do not also take a look at themselves.

The examination of self and organizations and the commitment to transformation is the essence of what Deming called a System of Profound Knowledge. The System of Profound Knowledge provides business leaders with insight into themselves and others. This insight is the cornerstone of building relationships with employees, customers, suppliers and consumers (not to mention family and friends). This leads to an understanding of life, events and interactions, all of which allow business and organizations to perform at their best.

For the business leader, this means setting a good example, being a good listener, being an educator and helping others to migrate away from current (nonproductive) practices and beliefs and to embrace a new philosophy without feeling guilty about the past. While the task seems daunting in a world of recession, bankruptcy and foreclosure, we cannot afford to operate our businesses, organizations and lives motivated by fear.

The truth is that fear and ego have transformed us from production powerhouses to stock symbols, logos and monetary appraisals. We do not need to be caught in this human-initiated downward spiral. Understanding what has worked in the past and what is possible in the future can make us economically viable again. Deming was a combination of sage and visionary, and what he developed as business truths a half-century ago have particular relevance in today's environment.

Deming's System of Profound Knowledge consists of four principles:

1. Appreciation of the organization (including suppliers, producers, employees, customers and consumers).

2. Knowledge of variation in cause and range of quality (by utilizing static sampling for measurement).

3. Theory of knowledge, which distinguishes what is applicable to the organization and what is ineffective.

4. Knowledge of psychology, the understanding of human nature.[4]

These principles are not individual steps and cannot be separated. All four are intermeshed. Nor is the System of Profound Knowledge merely theoretical. Dr. Deming's intent was to show companies how they could increase quality and customer loyalty while reducing costs and waste. To accomplish this goal, organizations must practice continual improvement and comprehend their businesses as overall (organic) systems

---

[4] The W. Edward Deming Institute. www.deming.org.

and not merely bits and pieces of various departments. Businesses are organic, much like the human bodyCa system that must be diagnosed and treated in order to function. For example, if an infection occurs on the palm, but only the hand is treated and the cause of the infection lies elsewhere untreated, the infection will fester and grow until the entire body is compromised.

Before introducing these principles into any organization, management must understand the distinction between information and knowledge. Information is task oriented while knowledge is an understanding of circumstances and possible outcomes. For example, when a child learns to tie her shoe, she is given the information to complete the task. Her knowledge is the understanding of what could happen if she does not complete her task properly, i.e., she could trip and fall. A person can synthesize information into knowledge to change conditions, and with added insight (i.e., wisdom), corrective action and continuous improvement can be made in any organization.

For a company to enact the Profound Knowledge, they must first realize that they are broken, and cannot be fixed by repeating what they have been doing over the past decades. The prescription for business is change. Management must be able to effectively communicate the need for change and the required information to enact change to employees throughout their organization in order for healing and operating from a place of well-being to begin. All healing takes time, which is why Deming advocated a long-term view. Rather than living and binging quarter-to-quarter, a healthy organization strives for long-term wellness from three to five years and beyond.

Management must be effective diagnosticians. Depending on circumstances at any given time in the business cycle, the following must be clearly understood:

What is the situation?

Whose role is it to respond?

When is the outcome needed?

What are the consequences of not meeting the need?

How will success be measured?

The information needs to be easily communicated, readily accessible, regularly updated and unambiguous.

While Deming is best known for his statistical models, his System of Profound Knowledge is organic in nature. This is because all organizations are made up of interdependent human beings; all businesses are, in essence, communities where success breeds success. The common vision that links everyone in the organization should be a continuous path to improvement.

Operating Bama Companies as a holistic entity means that not only does the company prosper, but that all members of our community thrive. We want employees to get a sense that they are empowered to do their best to overcome challenges. Through their participation in Bama they should know they are part of something important and that their contribution to the company's success is through helping others and being supported by others. They know that improvement is a continuous, never-ending process.

As Lewis A. Rhodes said in his article, "The Profound Knowledge School," Deming's System of Profound Knowledge provides the "know why" that makes "know how relevant."[5] Like a computer's operating system, it must be embedded deeply enough in the mind to be transparent. Employees, customers, consumers and the community at large all come with their own sets of beliefs and practices. All have developed knowledge based on information that has been part of their lives. The path to profound knowledge, and ultimately wisdom, requires adaptability and the willingness to make change. They must be willing to let go of the past, free themselves of what has not worked and embrace all that is possible.

"Before you can change what you do, you have to change how you think. Before you can change how you think, you have to change what you believe." But this is not an easy process for the "space" [mind] is already filled with a "program" [a set of beliefs] already developed from experience that have proved successful in the past."[6] Thus the learning process has to provide for an unlearning process, as part of work, that forces the questioning of assumptions and their

[5] Lewis. A. Rhodes. "The Profound Knowledge School," http://www. newhorizons.org/trans/rhodes.htm. 12/21/08 lewrhodes@aol.com.

[6] Ibid.

present consequences. A successful company gives employees the tools to embark on this process.

Process technologies, such as those found in quality management, identify the interdependence of roles within an organization so that they can be reinforced and become sustainable, supportive infrastructures. The application of The System of Profound Knowledge brings together individual pieces into one coherent process.

The coherent organization is dependent upon leadership with a vision that creates, aligns and sustains those relationships, and provides department and employees with ways for the parts of the system to act as an integrated system each and every day. This does not squelch individualism; rather, it provides a connectivity that allows the individuals within it to continually take advantage of their interdependence.

Such a coherent, connected approach is possible in any organization or society. Profound Knowledge makes it possible to achieve results utilizing a process that starts with the specific needs of the individual but expands to profound beliefs that lead to a common understanding and acceptance of why and how organizations are organically connected through the work of their parts and participants. To get to that level of awareness and quality requires that profound knowledge be developed through new forms of collaborative experience.

The System of Profound Knowledge is the basis for application of Dr. Deming's 14 Points for management listed below, which form not only the basis for this book but the day-in, day-out application of the Bama Companies:

1. Create constancy of purpose for the improvement of product and service with the aim to become competitive, stay in business and provide jobs.

2. Adopt a new philosophy of cooperation (win-win) in which everybody wins. Put it into practice and teach it to employees, customers and suppliers.

3. Cease dependence on mass inspection to achieve quality. Improve the process and build quality into the product in the first place.

4. End the practice of awarding business on the basis of price tag alone. Instead, minimize total cost in the long run. Move toward a single supplier for any one item, on a long-term relationship of loyalty and trust.

5. Improve constantly and forever the system of production, service, planning or any activity. This will improve quality and productivity and thus constantly decrease costs.

6. Institute training for skills.

7. Adopt and institute leadership for the management of people, recognizing their different abilities, capabilities and aspirations. The aim of leadership should be to help people, machines and gadgets do a better job.

Leadership of management is in need of overhaul, as well as leadership of production workers.

8. Drive out fear and build trust so that everyone can work effectively.

9. Break down barriers between departments. Abolish competition and build a win-win system of cooperation within the organization. People in research, design, sales and production must work as a team to foresee problems of production that might be encountered with the product or service.

10. Eliminate slogans, exhortations and targets asking for zero defects or new levels of productivity. Such exhortations only create adversarial relationships, as the bulk of the causes of low quality and low productivity belong to the system and thus lie beyond the power of the workforce.

11. Eliminate numerical goals, numerical quotas and management by objectives. Substitute leadership.

12. Remove barriers that rob people of joy in their work. This will mean abolishing the annual rating or merit system that ranks people and creates competition and conflict.

13. Institute a vigorous program of education and self-improvement.

14. Put everybody in the company to work to accomplish the transformation. The transformation is everybody's job.[7]

The common denominator in all of the points listed above is people.

[7] Phil Cohen. Deming's 14 Points, http://www.hci.com.au/hcisite2/articles/deming.html, 12/21/08.

CHAPTER TWO
CULTURAL INCLUSION

My grandmother, Cornilla Alabama "Bama" Marshall, started the Bama Pie Company in 1927. For eight decades the Bama Companies have operated with two principles in mind: 1.) Keep your eye on quality, and 2.) People make a company. What I have learned as the third generation owner of the company is that making our employees part of the Bama family not only contributes to the overall health of our organization, but also provides security and promise for everyone's future. We are seriously and sincerely committed to our employees' growth and personnel success. That commitment is returned in the implementation and sustenance of Deming's System of Profound Knowledge and productivity and quality through Six Sigma.

My mom, my friend and one of my business partners for the last thirty years also shares these philosophies. She is as tough as they come!! She listens, but she knows what she stands for ... Quality, Safety and People come first!! She has always supported my dad and me in all of our crazy endeavors.

She is ninety-two and still sits as the chairwoman of our organization ... she's a superstar!!

In 1988, Bama's Mission was formalized to capture the essence of its simple formula: The quality of Bama employees is in essence the formula for "quality" in our products and services.

Mission: People Helping People Be Successful.

Vision: Create and deliver loyalty, prosperity and fun for all stakeholders!!

When every member at every level of your corporate community embraces and follows the mission and vision of the company, the company itself is nurtured and continues to grow and prosper.

I take great pride that unleavened dough is the heart of our business. Unleavened dough has been the source of life for millennia. This symbolism is not lost in any member of the

Bama team as we strive not only to feed others but our spirits as well.

Deming's meteoritic rise in the public consciousness was a result of the work he headed up in the rebuilding of Japan's industry in the 1950s after World War II. The Japanese termed the cornerstone of their industrial philosophy "Kaizen." While he was credited with Japan's rebuilding efforts and received Japan's highest honors, Deming was quick to point out that he learned from the Japanese as well. The greatest lesson being that "people are important." The Kaizen business approach begins and ends with people.

Kaizen loosely translated means "gradual, orderly." In the business setting it is continual improvement that focuses on eliminating waste in all systems and processes of an organization. Success is dependent upon everyone in the organization working together to implement improvement without dependence on capital infusion. Kaizen is a top-down and bottom-up approach. Management guides everyone in the organization in the shared objective of high quality, low cost and on-time delivery of products and services.

Kaizen positively impacts the organization's entire culture by encouraging open communication, continual change, teamwork and taking personal responsibility for the day-to-day procedures one uses on the job.

Kaizen emphasizes action. At Bama, teams don't just sit in boardrooms pondering our problems or designing strategic plans; our people are out on the floor trying out new techniques until practical and effective ways to improve performance and meet customer expectations are found. Ours are not merely problem-solving teams; they are continuous improvement teams. This is an organic approach. By perceiving and appreciating Bama Companies as holistic, we nurture it to heal and grow. Problems are not surgically removed; the corporate body is encouraged to be healthy by continuously improving, stretching, growing, preventing and responding, always aware of our environment. Problems are allowed to surface and we do not hide them and just hope they will go away, or pass them on to the next department. Avoidance is costly to the bottom line. Bama has a "no blame" process where we emphasize everyone to be aware about problems before they become enormous and costly to customers, suppliers and ourselves. This is not accomplished by corporate edict or empty policy proclamations. Everyone shares a commitment for improvement through meaningful process development.

By creating a holistic process, employees are able to visually identify, analyze and assess the best solutions for any situation. If continuous improvement objectives are not being met, employees must return to the original process, revisit opportunities and provide alternative solutions. Analysis and diagnosis are critical to maintaining a healthy body. This cannot be achieved from a high level or the corporate corner office. Continuous improvement is achieved by breaking down difficult tasks into their sub or sub-sub components to make them more actionable.

There are five elements to this process.

1. Less is more: Eliminating steps in the process, eliminating unnecessary work or reducing the staffing level can help ensure improvement. For example, at Bama, a solution might involve using less manufacturing floor space for equipment and people.

2. Integration: To ensure new operations will fit into a company's production cycles or processes requires observation, counting, timing, measuring and diagramming the relevant steps of the process. Often, a new process method must be devised to reduce the inventory and to facilitate functional workflow.

3. Innovation: High-level ideas and hands-on problem-solving techniques must come together in interdepartmental teams. Teams are trained to interact and work together. Team members' responsibilities include creating agendas, keeping minutes, handling action items and focusing on the team mission. Teams are taught skills such as brainstorming, making checklists, diagrams and surveys and creating charts.

4. Inclusion: Although team building and teaching collaborative business skills are important to Kaizen, getting input from every employee is what makes it work. Kaizen philosophy asserts that every employee, regardless of education or experience, has valuable suggestions

to contribute. Diverse life experiences can also shed new light on problems.

5. Look beyond your own walls: Organizations exist to serve customers. Customer input regarding products or services is critical to identifying opportunities for continuous improvement. Ideas and skills for process improvement can come from many places. Rather than thinking of competitors as adversaries, many organizations find that they learn the most from studying their competitors to learn how to do things differently.

As a culture, we are accustomed to big, bold, robust gestures. But Kaizen recognizes that small, steady, incremental steps are the path to stimulating, motivating, exciting and continuously improving an organization. At Bama Companies it has become part of the very fabric of our company.

Creating a Kaizen culture isn't simple; it requires perseverance to transform a corporate culture. Through years of personal study and commitment, the Bama Companies have come to understand the goal is not the "best" way to do something; instead, all members of our business are empowered to continually look for a "better" way of doing things.

I have learned that the initiative must emanate from the CEO, who must demonstrate the passion, willingness and stomach to make a cultural shift. The CEO must have a steadfast commitment to invest in people and processes from the ground up. All employees need to embrace the shared vision and be dedicated to making continuous, incremental improvements.

First and foremost, Deming was a statistician. While one cannot measure the impact of culture in mathematical models, tools can be used that measure the effectiveness of adopting processes throughout the organization. The organization must maintain a consistent approach to track and monitor processes, ensuring proper review of the initiatives at site, regional and global levels.

As part of Bama's fundamentals to ensure continuous improvement, we have also established Kaizen workshops. These workshops begin weeks before any Kaizen event is to be initiated. This requires the project scope be outlined thoroughly and a cross-functional team formed to match project requirements. The team uses a methodology to generate as many possibilities for addressing the improvement opportunity. Each idea is assessed based on agreed criteria. The idea that has the highest score is then put into action through team interaction and brainstorming.

Again, it all comes back to people. By putting all situations on the table in the exact spot where issues occur, everyone sees the situation firsthand. This is done without fear of retribution; improvement is the intent. We find employees are then more apt to rally around the Kaizen event, better grasp the improvement opportunity and commit to fixing it to mutual satisfaction if they are not clouded by fear. Rather than "shooting the messenger," this is our opportunity to learn and grow. Those in management must understand that edicts contribute to the problems and to solutions.

Everyone from the CEO on through the organization must be willing to stand with the entire team and admit culpability when things go wrong.

In Bama, the Kaizen process has become so systematic that improvements are made much more efficiently. This approach keeps staff motivated and energized to seek out and implement further improvements.

Because suppliers and customers are part of the Bama family, improvements may be focused on a single line or, as in some cases, the improvement measures are within a facility. In other cases, the team will visit a supplier or a customer site and drive changes throughout the entire supply chain. All intervention is done with a culture committed to the process of improvement: a Kaizen culture.

This is as much a spiritual commitment as it is a business model. Leaders must create an environment where employees are empowered and rewarded for thinking of better ways to do things or results will stagnate and deployment will falter. An unfettered spirit soars; those who believe anything is possible will reach beyond any perceived constraints. A spiritual commitment is an endless commitment, not only to a particular organization but to our community, environment and universe.

New Factory – Beijing, China.

Some of the beautiful people I am privileged to work with.

Dr. Deming never called his theories spiritual, but I believe they are. By following his directives, leadership receives a spiritual awakening. Following Deming principles forces our egos to the backseat, and allows us to listen, respect, have compassion for and forgive others as we learn new tools for business.

Learn how nature works, and you will learn how to run a more harmonious business.

CHAPTER THREE
MEASURING THE CORPORATE EGO

We want our employees, suppliers, customers and consumers to feel pride in our organization. Pride is the happy, satisfied feeling we experience when having achieved something special. That something deserves admiration and respect.

Pride is satisfaction with no need to brag. However, ego is a more primordial thought process, impulsive and self-focused with a sense of superiority to others. Pride can be shared while ego is selfish and is often abusive.

A company that has a big ego doesn't like to admit failure. Executives in such a company will frequently go to great lengths so save face. The result: continuing programs and initiatives that aren't effective. The investment of energy and ideas that go into these programs creates an atmosphere that becomes self-protective. Accordingly, the program or initiative takes on a life of its own.

Companies with effective executives guide the culture of their organizations toward decreasing the ego levels of the individuals who are part of the company. Furthermore, a healthy look at the effectiveness of any program will result in identifying inefficient initiatives and making changes as appropriate.

The ego, more than any economic circumstance or process deficiency, can derail a business or organization. To remove the ego from business means "I am helping to remove it from me." To remove my ego and replace it with my soul means I can help my business do the same thing.

Ego is not a modern-day invention. It did not rise up out of the Industrial Revolution. Human beings have always worked this way. In ancient times, as populations grew, new "tribes" were formed. The dominating tribes would make new rules for all to follow. The spirits of some of the dominated, down-and-out, after being conquered, would eventually decide they did not like the new rules. No humans want to be conquered or enslaved or dominated. A few rebels became initiators; they banded together with others of like minds. They planned overthrows and new tribes. Most of the time these rebels were discovered by the dominating group and would be snuffed out with either force or coercion. Then, more warriors were brought in to squelch uprisings, and in turn, enacted more laws to squelch the rabble-rousers.

The ego can harm the organization, from arrogance to the compulsion to be right, from talking incessantly about the self to becoming attached to our own actions. However, if a CEO or any member of the organization believes "it is all about me," then their focus is not on the customer. Sometimes it is difficult to differentiate ego from pride or confidence. There are steps you can take to keep your ego in check. Alicia Smith, in her June 2006 Morebusiness.com article, recommends the following:

1. Maintain an open mind. When we come from a place of ego, we tend to be narrowly scoped. Usually we have difficulty seeing beyond what we can understand. We think we know the only way, that we have all of the answers. Business success, however, demands that we see the bigger picture. We must be open to new ideas, trends, opinions, and most importantly, to the variety of potential customers or clients with whom we'll undoubtedly interface. An open perspective may lead us to developing new and innovative products or programs. It may allow us to seek out others whom we might otherwise dismiss, possibly creating the opportunity for strategic business alliances or partnerships. An open mind opens us up to opportunities.

2. Listen more than you speak. It's been said that we were given two ears and one mouth so that we could listen twice as much as we speak. While there is definitely merit to this statement, it really goes one step deeper. Almost every single time we speak, we are speaking from a place of ego. We are talking about ourselves, something we saw, something we did,

something we have an opinion about. While that is all good and fine, when it comes to business we need to make some adjustments.

Business is about serving the needs of others, specifically your target market. It's all about them. To be successful, you need to listen to what they say. What are their biggest problems, needs, and desires? What are they looking for you to do for them? How can your products or services solve their problems? The only way to determine that is by listening closely and carefully. When you speak, come from a place of inquiry and curiosity. And, make sure that everything you speak about relates back to the client in some way.

3. Serve others instead of ourselves. Most of us are in business to make money. That end is worthy and necessary to meet our goal of making a living. But, in order to create a successful business, our orientation must be from the standpoint of serving others. It is by serving others that we serve ourselves. Of all of the business blunders, this is probably the one that leads the way to slow growth or to eventual business failure. Each day we need to evaluate our activities. Certainly we must handle various administrative and operational tasks for our business.

But, aside from these, all other activities need to be focused around serving our clients. Ask yourself the question: Is what I'm doing serving or going to serve the needs and requirements of my clientele? If the answer is "no," reevaluate why you are doing it. You may be wasting time, money and energy pursuing activities that will have no value. Orient everything you do around serving others and you'll naturally end up serving yourself as well.

4. Practice humility. Humility or the state of being humble is an absolute must in business, for no matter what we do in life, there will always be times when we cannot control what is happening around us or to us. By developing an attitude of gratitude and being thankful in the moment for things going well, we'll be able to weather the storm much better when things go awry. Practicing humility means that we must face our own failures and imperfections. It also means that we must know our place when it comes to dealing with others—that we must treat others as we would like to be treated. It demands that we set aside our ego and realize that we are no better and no worse than anyone else; that we are on our own path that is unique to us and for us. There is no place for ego in a humble heart.

5. Don't get attached to outcomes. Being attached to outcomes is a surefire path to disappointment and a waste of our mental energies. It is our ego that fuels our intense desire to create specific outcomes. And, just like clockwork, this type of attitude leads to

disappointment when the desired outcome fails to manifest. No one can control the outcome of a situation. All we can do is make decisions based on the best data possible. There are a myriad of intervening circumstances that can derail even the best of plans. For this reason, it's important to set aside our egos and understand we only have so much power to steer our course. We need to develop a sense of peace that we have made the best decisions based upon what we know and leave it at that.

6. Avoid perfection. A big ego usually accompanies an attitude that everything has to be perfect. Perfect is an impossible idealism that keeps people from moving forward and accomplishing all that they can. Perfection will prevent you from giving a speech because you don't think it's good enough. Perfection will stop you from writing a book, making a phone call to a prospect or presenting a tele-class on a topic you love. Don't let this unproductive attitude invade your life. It's rooted in ego—a need to be right, a need to be better than others and beyond reproach. Ironically, most people are not drawn to perfectionists, as they are often perceived as uptight, unrealistic and better than everyone else. Your clients will be drawn to you because of who you areCfailures, mistakes, and imperfectionsCthe whole nine yards. People will seek you out because you are a real

personCsomeone they can identify with. Don't let perfection stand in the way of being who you are.

7. Make mistakes. Mistakes are a part of life. And really, there are no mistakes; there are only experiences. Experiences provide us with feedback that allow us to make other decisions that lead us towards what we want to accomplish. If we aren't willing to have experiences, we aren't going to have a life or a business for that matter. A big ego will often prevent us from having experiences because it perceives that a "mistake" is a bad thing and a sign of failure. The funny thing about this is that you're probably the only one who notices the mistake, as other folks are much too busy being concerned with their own lives. Get out of yourself, shed your ego and start living. The most successful business owners are the ones who step out, have experiences and fail their way to success.

8. Be right, not righteous. There's a big difference between being right and being righteous. Being righteous is all about your ego. You think that you have a monopoly on "right"; that you know and have all the answers; and that everyone who does not believe as you do is wrong. Righteous folks are frightened folks. Often they are raised on fear-based ideas put forth by otherwise well-meaning parents or institutions. They are wrapped up in their own world, unaware of other people. They don't know how to respect others

because they themselves harbor nothing worthy of respect. After all, it's ludicrous to believe anyone has a monopoly on truth or what is right. Still, you may see this creeping into your own approach to business. Whenever you feel the need to express righteousness, know that it's your ego rearing its ugly head.

9. Consult others. Seeking out counsel, information, wisdom or feedback from others is a wonderful way to bring creativity, inspiration and motivation to all that you do. If your ego were in play, you wouldn't even consider such a thing. Ego is all about you. You don't have a place for others, their ideas or their feedback. Business is all about interfacing with others, from your colleagues, to your vendors and supplies, to your all-important customers or clients. Just like with the idea of "having an open mind," tremendous opportunity can come your way by consulting with others. Don't close down the doors to success. Instead, open them wide by setting aside your ego and connecting with others.

10. Let others tell your story. Why not completely take you and your ego out of the picture and let others speak for you. Testimonials and referrals are, by far, the most powerful tools you can use to build your business. People relate to the stories that others tell them. They hold much more credibility than if you were to talk about yourself and your client successes.

Actively gather testimonials from the folks you do business with. Make sure to include a few of them in your various marketing materials. Post them on your website for everyone to view and read. If someone says wonderful things about you but is uncomfortable writing a testimonial, offer to transcribe what they tell you and then send it to them for final approval.[8]

In these ten basic steps, Alicia Smith has articulated the keys to organizational success.

Unfortunately, these principles are not taught in most executive MBA programs. Because we live in and ego-driven culture, it is not hard to understand why our schools and thus our corporations fall into the self-serving, ego-driven practice of numbers and greed. But we can do better by showing our employees and suppliers there is a better, more humane way to transact business.

Organization transformation begins with the executives' sincere desire to move from being ego-driven, to a state of "seeing" the perfection in each and every soul, regardless of their power or status.

The process for this type of transformation is not easy; it requires rehabilitation from the ego's addictive control over each person in each phase of the chain of operation. Customer/supplier

---

[8] Alicia Smith. "The Business Ego Trap: Having an Ego in Business," Morebuiness.com, June 5, 2006.

relationships, shareholder relations, financial processes, business systems, compensation systems and the current set of operating philosophies, all which govern Wall Street, the investor community and the American and international workplace, are in need of an ego overhaul.

The ego is reliant upon external motivation for every decision that is made. External motivation, in the form of cash, stocks, options and any other type of compensation are used to influence behavior in all types of work environment. The ego is self-motivated and as a result keeps its focus on money first, fast-paced growth, fast-paced profits for instant financial gratitude. Business is addicted to this state of "urgency," while ego believes everything is needed now! Because everything is important, nothing is important.

This is typical of today's business practices. Upper managers bring in more middle managers to "oversee" the work of others. There is no value added; they exist just to keep people in line. In business these overseers are called "audit" departments. After the first line of audits occur, new auditors are brought in to audit the auditors, so people are kept in line by fear rather than motivated to improve.

Since people become scared of doing things wrong, fear and intimidation mean approximately 80 percent will comply with current decisions, 10 percent will look for expedient (not necessarily effective) decisions and 10 percent will jump ship. Fear discourages dissension and thus innovation; therefore, for most people the job becomes a chore, a joyless act. Going to work becomes an endless cycle of unhappiness. Ego has conquered ego. Those at the top have ego-based power leaving those below to have to choose in order to save their jobs and ultimately well-being. While human beings are hardwired, ego-based beings, one thing can prevail over ego: community.

Everyone deeply desires community. No matter how hermetically sealed our lives may be, no matter how much we cherish our personal space, no matter how "burned" we may feel by past experiences with groups, something in us aches for the experience of authentic belonging. Community is an archetype imbedded in the human psyche regardless of culture or ethnicity. In America, as perhaps no other place or period in history, this archetype has been disowned in favor of bootstrap pulling and "doing it my way."

It is useful to recall that all of us are descendants of tribal peoples whose lives revolved around and were shaped moment-to-moment by community. I believe that an ancient memory of tribal life—the good, the bad and everything in between—exists within us.

Community evokes a group of trusted friends sitting around a table; a gathering of families on Thanksgiving or friends enjoying a concert. But community is more than pleasantries. Tribal cultures over the millennia have been forced to create community for the same reasons we must as we confront global warming, global economic collapse and other worldwide threats. Our ancestors had to cope with earthquakes, floods, packs of hungry animals, plagues, fires, famine and rival warring tribes; the earliest humans banded together in communities as a matter of necessity. Survival dictated cooperation—just as it most certainly will in the years to come. We must work in community as we struggle for survival. We must temper our egos and reject the negative states of mind such as anger, resentment, fear, envy and jealousy, which are also products of the ego. If together we move toward continuous improvement rather than a number, a sense of shared well-being and hope can prevail and success can be shared.

As business and organizational leaders, we must foster a sense of community within our organizations. At the Bama Companies we know people make everything work. When people feel that the organization gives back to them as much as they are giving to the organization, they are willing to give more. People Helping People is the mission of the Bama Companies.

CHAPTER FOUR

AVOIDING THE CONTAMINATED CULTURE

History is rife with fallen cultures, from the ancient Greeks and Mayans to Enron and Lehman Brothers. All failed societies, corporations, organizations and governments fell because they allowed the culture to become contaminated. Greed, ego, envy and fear are lethal contaminants. People contribute when they feel valued and respected. Employees perform well when they are appreciated. Self-worth has greater intrinsic value than financial worth, yet throughout Western businesses and organizations, the bottom line is the only metric that has been guiding CEOs, senior management and Human Resource Departments.

Researcher, business leader, motivational speaker and trainer Marcus Buckingham has been writing about the significance of employee job satisfaction for more than a decade. The responses to the twelve-point questionnaire he developed decades ago as a senior researcher for the Gallup Organization provides insight into how well a team or community in any organization will perform.

1. Do I know what is expected of me at work?

2. Do I have the materials and equipment that I need in order to do my work right?

3. At work, do I have the opportunity to do what I do best every day?

4. In the past seven days, have I received recognition or praise for doing good work?

5. Does my supervisor, or someone at work, seem to care about me as a person?

6. Is there someone at work who encourages my development?

7. At work, do my opinions seem to count?

8. Does the mission or purpose of my company make me feel that my job is important?

9. Are my coworkers committed to doing quality work?

10. Do I have a best friend at work?

11. In the past six months, has someone at work talked to me about my progress?

12. This past year, have I had opportunities at work to learn and grow?[9]

---

[9] Marcus Buckingham. *First, Break All the Rules; Now, Discover Your Strengths,* 233.

What Buckingham learned is that companies that focus on cultivating all employees' strengths, regardless of job grade, rather than chastising them for their weaknesses, receive the dual benefit of satisfied, motivated personnel and increased organizational efficiency.

When employees do not perform to organizational expectation, all too often senior management and Human Resource Departments blame the workers for the failure. But it is the organization that holds the blame. Too often policies are perceived as arbitrary, unclear and inequitable. Penalties are emphasized instead of rewards.

It is not unusual to hear CEOs and Human Resource Departments contend that they want their employees to "work smarter, not harder." Few of them understand that people cannot and will not work smarter when they have supervisors hovering over them, dictating and measuring their every move. They especially will not work harder or smarter if management has defined the ultimate goal to be a bottom line enterprise as they soar like hawks over their organizations hunting for jobs to eliminate and people to lay off. People everywhere will work smarter and harder for the customer, but they will not work harder for someone who has defined them as a "variable cost."

Employees want to believe and be recognized for their contributions. They must comprehend that the work they are doing is important and that their tasks are meaningful. Their contributions should not be taken for granted. At Bama we make it a point to share stories of success and about how an employee's actions made a real difference in making our process better. We know the importance of making a "big deal" out of meaningful tasks that may have become ordinary. Even the mundane has value. Granted, employees may not find all their tasks interesting or rewarding, but there should be acknowledgement to the employee as how those tasks are essential to the overall processes that make the organization succeed. Through their contributions, input and knowledge, certain tasks that truly are unnecessary can be identified and eliminated or streamlined, resulting in greater efficiency and satisfaction.

The fact is that people take pride in doing good work. People succeed when they are placed in positions that utilize their talents and encourage their success and do not set them up for failure. Positive feedback and recognition are powerful compensation.

Individuals at all levels of the organization want to be recognized for their achievements on the job. Their successes don't have to be monumental to deserve recognition. Praise, however, cannot be window dressing; it must be sincere. If you notice employees doing something well, you should take the time to acknowledge their good work immediately. Publicly thank them for handling a situation particularly well. Have managers, supervisors and Human Resource personnel catching people doing their jobs well, not on the hunt for what people are doing wrong.

Employees continue to be motivated to do their jobs well if they have ownership of their work. This requires giving employees enough freedom and power to carry out their tasks so that they feel they "own" the result. As individuals mature in their jobs, we provide opportunities for added responsibility, always mindful that the intent is not to simply add more work. The objective is find ways to add challenging and meaningful work, perhaps even giving the employee greater freedom and authority as well. Ownership is part of the pride people take in their work. The pride is part of the overall community, the culture of the Bama Companies.

Whether it's in society or business, the existing culture is composed of the common underlying values by which the participants coexist as they do business. A strong, clearly articulated culture brings cohesiveness to the organization and becomes a source of pride. To quote motivational speaker, Dr. Lewis Losoncy, Come-*unity* creates oppor-*unity*. If every teammate knows, for example, that his or her culture believes in and values "exceeding customer expectations," the team proceeds as one and sends a clear message to the consumer.[10]

Maintaining a successful business requires a cohesive culture whose members feel they are part of a secure, worthwhile community. That community has the ability to motivate its members to exceptional performance. Community can set standards of expectations for individuals and provide a climate in which great things happen.[11]

---

[10] Lewis Losoncy. *The Motivating Team Leader,* DC Press, Sandford, Florida, xxii.

[11] J. Thomas. Wren. *The Leader's Companion: Insights on Leadership Through the Ages,* Free Press, 1995, 501.

The Bama Companies ensure a contaminant-free culture by maintaining a set of core principles.

1. Respect. Our community encourages an atmosphere of mutual understanding and respect for every member of the organization, regardless of their role.

2. Building up. Our community motivates and strives for improvement by providing positive input and feedback. Managers and coworkers are expected to build people up, not tear them down.

3. Value of purpose. Everyone at every level in our community knows they are of value to us. Confidence in their abilities is expressed and they are appreciated for their efforts.

4. Optimism. Our community expects members to take chances and face challenges realistically. Everyone is encouraged to honor their better selves by using the unlimited potential of their creative minds to solve problems and continuously improve.

5. Involvement. Our community expects everyone to participate. Cooperation is emphasized over competition.

6. Commitment. Continuous improvement is a continuous commitment to developing the skills, attitudes, pride, productivity, creativity and involvement of everyone in the community.

Community is a natural state. Human beings want to belong to a social unit. They want to feel included and inclusive. Pride comes from the opportunity to contribute and share ourselves with others. Unfortunately, most businesses are designed around artificial models, not around the natural human state. However, everything we need to know to create a successful business is modeled in infancy. As Losoncy says, "Business leaders have a powerful ally. They have no less than human nature on their side."[12]

Babies are born with a sense of wonder and the instinct to be a part of the world around them. Over the years as society chastises children, criticizes their creativity and makes them fearful of their curiosity, they become repressed. But those inborn tendencies to be creative can be reignited in a contaminant-free culture. Babies do not want to be isolated; they want to (need to) be part of a family, a nurturing community. Children respond to positivity and shrink away from negativity; these innate responses are no different in adults. Punishment and pay are not motivators. Only self-worth ensures long-term commitment to the community or culture.

One-person companies are nonexistent. According to *Webster's Dictionary*, a company is a number of persons associated for some common purpose.[13] This is synonymous with

---

[12] Lewis Losoncy. *The Motivating Team Leader.* Sanford, Florida, 2003, 27.

[13] *The New International Webster's Concise Dictionary of the English Language,* Trident International, 1998, 143.

the concept of a community. At Bama, we understand that most employees spend more of their waking hours each week at the workplace than they do with their family members or friends. Therefore, it is our responsibility to ensure there is a solid sense of community within our corporation and that is achieved through equity. We are structured such that people are focused on their core roles at work rather than on a particular position or hierarchy. This allows everyone to feel a part of the culture.

While committed to employees' sense of well-being, this is not just a purely egalitarian approach; multiple studies show that companies and organizations with an engaged workforce have greater productivity and retention. People who have more fun and believe there is equity in the organization support each other and cooperate with each other. These positive relationships cultivate finding solutions rather than being focused on accessing blame. This positivity is a critical factor in continuous improvement.

Relationships cannot be built in isolation. People must actually talk with one another and cannot depend simply on reports, memos and e-mails to communicate. Finger-pointing, blame and stagnation result when people don't talk face-to-face or interact in other ways. Interaction allows for camaraderie, even friendship. When you are willing to look out for another person, a person whom you consider a friend, you are more willing to take on responsibility and accountability that ensure everyone's success. To quote John W. Gardner, "Embracing and promoting a product is one thing," he said, "but when you nurture people you encourage their personal growth and fulfillment, and your return on investment is greater productivity."[14]

Corporate performance is not a singular event. Employees, customers and consumers must remain engaged day after day, week after week and year after year. The key is to keep participants from becoming apathetic or dispirited while keeping morale high. This is accomplished by being goal oriented rather than ego oriented.

An ego-centered operation is most often a hierarchy where individual ideas and suggestions loom. The individual egos won't allow anyone else making suggestions or taking credit. Blame is singled out. Motivation is through reward and punishment (usually monetary).

A goal-centered organization is focused on continuous improvement rather than individual credit or blame. What matters to the organization is that the best, most efficient and most enjoyable way of doing the job and satisfying the customer are used. The individual source of the idea is not equated with the value of the idea. The goal is what is best for the customer and the consumer.

The redirection of focus is healthy for the organization, the employees, the customers, the consumers and the larger community beyond the corporate walls. For example, in an ego-centered organization, if there is a personality or personnel

---

[14] J. Thomas Wren. *On Leadership: Insights on Leadership Through the Ages,* Free Press, 1995, 294.

difference, the tendency is to respond with punishment or an act of revenge. Getting even takes precedence. However, in a goal-centered organization, the well-being of the community is the focus. Everyone understands that the organization's success is linked to personal well-being. Individual conflicts and differences are put aside and people work together to find what is best for everyone involved.

At the Bama Companies we know the only way to be a goal-centered organization rather than an ego-centered organization is to foster and promote listening. There must be a willingness to listen to the ideas of all people, regardless of position. Everyone understands they must listen to each other whether they like or dislike the person with the recommendation. Suggestions and contributions all have value regardless of the person making them.

Change is a constant and should not be resisted. Continuous improvement rejects the status quo and welcomes the challenges of innovation. An ego-centered organization demands perfection and punishes for mistakes made. A goal-centered organization strives for improvement, champion risk takers, and strives to learn from mistakes and missteps. If people are afraid to fail, they will keep ideas to themselves and opportunities may be missed. Therefore, Bama has developed the following mind-set for encouraging the sharing of ideas:

1. No ideas are wrong. All innovations were once novel ideas that seemed impossible. The worst case is that an idea is not usable now.

2. There are multiple ways to look at challenges and changes. Most often there is not a single "right way" to do things.

3. Solutions require uniqueness and creativity. An individual's unique perspective may lead to an answer that may have been missed; diversity must be embraced.

4. The value of an idea is not based upon who suggested it but on its ability to work and provide benefit to the community.

5. Sharing all ideas is beneficial. Some ideas have value to particular situations while others have merit because they generate additional ideas.

6. There is no bad time for a good idea. As long as employees are willing to share their ideas without fear of judgment, innovations and continuous improvement will prevail.

The overall philosophy is that by supporting each other we can do much more together than each of us can do alone, since internal competition divides us. Our shared destiny builds on our individual strength and provides all of us an opportunity to succeed. This approach does not squelch individualism; rather, it honors people's natural need as social beings and fulfills their need to belong. Pride is instilled for both the self and the community. The self and the community are empowered in achieving a common goal made up of common interests and the desire for continuous improvement. Success and achievement are better appreciated when celebrated with others.

Not only is the organization fortified, but everyone obtains and maintains a greater appreciation of their coworkers, their roles within the organization and everyone's place in the world. This is the essence of spirit and energy.

My mentor, Dr. Deming, knew that human beings are made up of energy. He understood science and physics.. Atomically he knew how the universe worked and he applied his theories to business. He knew joy is an individual thing and that each person must pursue it for himself or herself. He knew it could not be measured into someone, nor could it be exchanged or prostituted for money. He knew money would contaminate. He was a brilliant, Ph.D. in statistics. Although he was a "science" guy, he was Spirit-filled.

He preached day after day, seminar after seminar, to people who often ridiculed and laughed at him. He concerned himself with shifting quality and variation in processes. He knew there were millions of dollars of cost buried in financial statements and much waste in traditional systems. Ultimately, he spent his entire life working with the Japanese to help them improve their economy and their businesses, that allowed them to become global powerhouses with products and services of the highest quality and the lowest possible costs. Today, the Japanese have such a superior understanding of quality that others globally want to emanate them. The Japanese have come to understand variation as it relates to the processes needed to produce consistent quality. While they utilize statistical process control and data to make decisions, their understanding of spirit and energy also matters to the business model. Everything in life is a system, which contains variation. The physical universe we live in is constantly changing.

Every living organism is an energetic, magnetic, pulsating, shifting and changing mass. In a business environment, patterns of energy shift minute by minute, hour by hour and day by day. Business is made up of human beings, so it makes perfect sense that the life cycles of the organization and the individual are similar. Life cycles are a part of our existence. They are completely natural and predictable through time. Although in business the cycles may seem harder to define, they do exist and anticipating them rather than responding to the unexpected emergency will allow the energy of business to flow with the energy of the universe.

All business managers have a choice. They can operate out of urgency, driven by fear and ego or they can harness the positive energy of their personnel to not just solve immediate problems but to grow and continuously improve their organizations.

Management today spends such a large percentage of its time on Wall Street expectations and monthly and quarterly projections that there is little time left for running the business. So much time and money are spent on acquiescing the desires of disengaged shareholders and business analysts that the organism that is the business is ignored and not nurtured.

Much is debated about how much financially to invest in various businesses. Now is the time to reinvest ourselves and the power of the human spirit into our enterprises. Only the energy of the human spirit can breathe life into a faltering organism. All human beings have an innate desire to matter to someone, something, sometime. Through innate desire and energy we can rebuild and improve our organizations into something that matters to the employee, customer, consumer and greater community. Allowing others to utilize their heart, soul, mind and body at work is natural, positive and eternal, and will allow companies to perform at their peak.

We will learn to work in harmony with one another on a local and global basis. As a result, products will have fewer and fewer defects and costs of operation will be lower. Absenteeism will be drastically reduced and people will come to work motivated to help one another. These are the keys to true prosperity.

CHAPTER FIVE
ORGANIC LEADERSHIP

Too often CEOs are focused on the bottom line, the share price or the latest Wall Street analysis. Reporting statistics and share earnings does not qualify a manager as a leader. The most important qualification of a business leader is the ability to motivate, empower and encourage an organization's employees.

Instead of projections, calculations and forecasts, in order to be effective, business leaders are going to have to exhibit the ability to elicit courage, hope, compassion, listening, cooperation and service from the workforce. Instead of constantly pointing out what people are doing wrong and not accomplishing, the true leader strives to bring out the best in people.

The core of the word "encourage" is courage. One of the greatest leaders of the twentieth century, Winston Churchill, said, "Courage is the first of human qualities because it is the quality which guarantees all others."[15] The greatest courage of all is the willingness to put aside our own egos for the greater good of the organization. The ability to put aside your ego means you are willing to put your trust and belief in others. When others sense you believe in them, they are willing to be optimistic about their own abilities and standards. This creates positive expectations and intrinsic motivation. Employees feel empowered and motivated to take action.

A trusted workforce that is heard and respected becomes uplifted. This shared vision allows them to act, think and perform differently. They are willing to support and sustain each other. This shared optimism is only possible when the owners, CEOs and managers sincerely believe in the people in their organizations and motivate them to be creative and take action for the benefit of the organization, customers, consumers and the community at large. Setbacks and downturns are understood as temporary situations rather than seen as personal failures that need to be punished.

An effective leader trusts in people's higher selves and their natural willingness to contribute to one another. Such leaders are able to define, articulate and reinforce the organization's culture. A shared culture is a source of pride for the members of the culture and they understand this creates opportunity for everyone. This cohesive culture comes from a shared vision. The organization's leader is the one best able to articulate this vision.

---

[15] Winston Churchill. *Bartlett' s Familiar Quotations*, Sixteenth edition, Little Brown and Co.,1992, 712:9.

While this might seem a new approach to management since organic leadership is not taught in business schools, this approach to leadership is as old as time. The history of humankind is the tribe. Within their tribes they shared season festivals, spiritual celebrations and the milestones of life cycles. This shared appreciation helps cultures work together and that need exists in every corporation and organization in the twenty-first century.

But not only do people need to be part of culture, they also need to express themselves through imagination and creativity. The effective leader honors both the social needs and the creative needs of individuals within their organizations. By modeling how to put ego aside, people are able to use their energies in constructive, positive ways and better avoid defensive and destructive behaviors.

It is the "leader" (CEO, owner, president or business manager) who establishes the organization's pride, trust, creativity, involvement, productivity and commitment by sincerely believing in the possibility of a harmonious environment. They provide their organizations with meaning and purpose beyond the paycheck or bottom line. Often the greatest motivation a leader can give is, "I believe in you; I believe in us."

At the Bama Companies, a leader possesses the following criteria:

1. Willing to listen to others.

2. A belief that everyone in the organization wants to make a contribution.

3. Positive, optimistic attitude towards others and an interest in their well-being.

4. A conscious effort to point out what others do correctly.

5. Willing to involve input from others and be open to diverse ideas.

6. Sees mistakes as an opportunity to correct and improve operations.

7. Motivates through encouragement and appreciation.

8. Focuses on cooperation instead of competition.

9. Appreciates how others perceive situations instead of just my own point of view.

10. Recognizes that people take pride in their work when they feel good about themselves and what they are doing.

These ten principles are the foundation for communication, understanding and mutual respect among all people within an organization. This results in positive energy.

The harmonious organization is not happenstance; it is the result of intentional leadership and sincere understanding of all participants. Empathy and understanding build trust and eliminate fear that comes from judgment. Leaders understand that the success of their organizations is directly related to the strength and energy of their personnel.

When individuals are encouraged to gain knowledge and make contributions, they are more creative and less defensive. As a result, they perform at a higher level than those who are torn down by blame and criticism. People live up to the expectations projected on them. Studies have shown that self-image or self-esteem may better determine a person's professional achievement than their I.Q.[16]

The organic leader also recognizes that the people in their organizations are complex individuals serving multiple roles in their lives. They are spouses, parents, children and caretakers. They have hobbies and interests. They participate in clubs and civic and religious organizations. By listening to them and understanding who they are completely, the leader can further assess their talents and get a better understanding of what motivates them. Everything about their lives is significant; the work environment should be a reflection of that wholeness, not a begrudging interruption. This applies to people in every task and level of the organization.

People follow what you do, not what you say. They sense apathy and disappointment as keenly as any child. Your staff looks to you for inspiration and positive purpose. Never miss an opportunity to give public and private credit to the idea

---

[16] William Purkey. *Psycho-Cybernetics: Self-Concept and School Achievement*, Prentice Hall, 1970, www.hypnosisclinic.com.au/hypnosis-subliminal-message-reference.html.

givers and contributors from every task and level in the organization. Continue to communicate your belief in them and your shared purpose.

At the Bama Companies we understand that ideas and contributions are in direct relation to delegation. More than being told what to do, our people feel respected when we trust them, train them and give them the responsibility to get things done. We celebrate their achievements. Delegation requires a certain level of risk taking, but we have discovered that over the long run as people grow and become responsible for more of the operation, the total organization grows and prospers. If I know that my employees know as much as they can about their jobs and the company, then I can focus on new issues.

Delegation cannot be done haphazardly. It involves analyzing the people throughout the organization to see who is

trained and capable of taking on certain responsibilities and who should be trained.

Challenges, problems and conflicts will continue to occur in any organization. Consequences occur when leaders refuse to recognize that problems exist. Problems are an opportunity to set an example and teach others how to deal with conflict. A leader does not motivate their organization by allowing unproductive or irresponsible behavior to reside within the organization.

The organic leader not only recognizes negative conditions but addresses them by recognizing why they occur:

What is the root cause for a person not feeling fulfilled or respected?

What is the root cause for a person or department not to feel motivated?

What outside factors may be impacting a person's performance?

Is the root cause due to lack of proper training?

What can we do to help or improve a situation?

When leaders fail to recognize or analyze problems, the entire organization is impacted and motivation will wane throughout. People will doubt a leader's sincerity and commitment not only if one area is heaped in praise above others, but if particular areas of concern are ignored or not addressed. The organic leader is aware that a positive, healthy balance needs to be maintained for the organization to thrive. Imbalances need to be corrected.

Most people have a negative response to the word "confrontation." But the actual definition of "confront" is "to face." By facing issues as they arise, the organic leader has the opportunity to teach and correct rather than blame and criticize. Facing these challenges allows people to gather facts and alternate views as to the source of the problem while informing and educating. The basis of confronting a situation should be the underlying belief that dealing with a problem is more effective than allowing it to continue, as long as the goal is to maintain balance within the organization.

Not facing challenges is synonymous with allowing a disease to fester in your organization. Each day the symptoms become more pronounced, but fear of a diagnosis keeps the leader from facing the illness. Balance is replaced with anxiety. Treatment is the path to healing. To confront (face), with the goal to educate, motivate and heal, is a positive act which includes:

1. Gathering the facts.

2. Willingness to listen.

3. Recognizing the assets, strengths and resources as well as the issue.

4. Avoiding anger and blame and maintaining respect.

5. Offering corrective action.

Just as with illness, some actions can be preventative. Operating guidelines represent preventative action. Defining procedures and guidelines, rather than being restrictive, are actually freeing to the organization because they maintain balance. With organizational direction, people do not have to guess at what is expected. Guessing causes imbalance.

Bama's preventative actions include:

1. Customer satisfaction is our main purpose.

2. Willingness to listen.

3. Every employee at every task and every level is important.

4. Expectations are clearly stated.

5. Each person knows what they are responsible for within the organization.

6. We value and respect competence, improvement and desire.

7. We respect each other by acting responsibly and working together.

Problems and issues may occur when the leader has not clarified the roles, responsibilities, rights and obligations of the participants. These factors need to be adjusted and reiterated to fit where the organization is in its life cycle. Assumption is the root cause of many problems; clarification is preventative medicine.

It is relatively easy to be a leader when things are going well and profits are up. An effective leader is one who can continue to motivate personnel during difficult times because he or she is focused on finding solutions and knows that the people within the organization are the ones who can find a path to solutions. The organization knows that every suggestion will be considered and that progress is as appreciated as outcome. Employees feel safe to brainstorm and recommend various options because they are in a work environment that encourages diverse thinking and multiple approaches to challenges.

The organic leader knows that every person in the organization is a stepping-stone on the path towards a solution. The more people are encouraged to participate, the shorter the journey to results.

It is essential that leaders do not shy away from issues or deny their existence. They see the situations for what they are and understand what events and circumstances they can affect. In work and in life, the organic leader surrounds themselves with positive, uplifting, solution-oriented people. They harness energy and do not fall victim to it.

People are not born disenfranchised, apathetic and uncooperative. The natural state is to want to create, belong and contribute. People who are disrespected and put down become disinterested or rebellious; their egos become their defense. Those who are not trusted become distrustful of others. Every religion has a version of the Golden Rule, which is to treat people the way you want to be treated. This is a universal principle. Following this basic truth allows the organic leader to encourage employees to focus on situations and solutions rather than on individual egos. What matters to all members of an organization is that the best, most efficient way of accomplishing things is utilized.

The source of the idea has nothing to do with the value of the idea since everyone wants to incorporate the best idea because the organization's success leads to everyone's individual success. It allows everyone to feel part of the whole while satisfying their individual needs to belong and contribute and have pride. Remember, a shared culture:

1. Shares a common goal. Common interests unite individuals.

2. Allows for greater individual involvement and a shared understanding of each person's role and how they fit into the culture.

3. Allows for cooperation and mutual encouragement and respect.

Organic leaders think in terms of the organization's culture and not their own ego or desires. They stay focused on the greater whole and not the self. Although much is heralded in this country, competition actually creates more losers than winners.

It is natural for losers to become defensive by blaming and making excuses and alienating themselves from the perceived winner. Motivating the organization through cooperation is a more effective approach to developing and respecting everyone in the organization.

Today, more than ever witnessed before, leadership is in dire need of change. What will give us courage and motivate us to inspire change in our organizations? It takes courage to put individual egos aside and break the addiction focused on numbers and legal maneuverings. How will we choose to respond to current events of a continually worsening economy? How will we choose to change the direction of current day management structures? Will we become organic leaders through choice or crisis?

Cooperation brings all the available resources into the organization's quest for continuous improvement. The organization shares pride and celebrates all achievements made by working in harmony. We define it at Bama this way: Success is not the product of individuals, but by people working together to create products and services, which help our customers improve their lives.

Once a CEO makes the decision to be an organic leader, they become a positive force and gain a huge advantage over negative energy. The truth is, no worthwhile human achievement has ever occurred out of pessimism or cynicism. Every worthwhile accomplishment from curing polio to man walking on the moon happened as the result of optimistic, motivated, inspired people working together, supporting one another, creating long-term, lasting relationships among individuals, work groups, suppliers and customers.

Any business, organization or government leader can be the organic leader, the person willing to put ego aside and empower others, motivating them with the endless possibilities of continuous improvement.

CHAPTER SIX

INTENTIONAL LISTENING

There are no one-person companies. Every organization is dependent upon people not only working together, but supporting each other. In most business, self-help and relationship books, communication is identified as the number-one required skill. Communication has become a cliché. Everyone is eager to communicate—speak their mindCbut what is needed throughout any enterprise is intentional listening. The focus is not what I have to say; rather, it should be, "Who am I hearing?"

In Western culture, it is not uncommon for people to talk to each other, but not actually listen to what the other person is saying. Because our lives are so busy, we are often distracted, our minds thinking about something else. This is exacerbated when tension or conflict exists. Rather than paying attention to what is being expressed, the tendency is to formulate a response, wait for silence and then respond not to what was being said but with how the respondent can win the argument.

An intentional listener purposefully attends to the speaker, digests their words and considers what has been said. A successful listener is able to clear their mind so they can be receptive to what is being said. One tactic is to repeat the speaker's words or intentions back before offering a response. This ensures what the listener heard is what the speaker intended to say. An intentional listener is not required to agree with the speaker; attention and respect are not acquiescence, but are the cornerstones of understanding.

There are several benefits to intentional listening. The most obvious is that it avoids misunderstandings. When people know that they are being heard, they become less defensive and are more willing to be open and trusting with others in their organization. Conflicts can be minimized, leaving more time to focus on continuous improvement.

To be an intentional listener requires you to be honest with yourself and aware of what is causing distractions in your mind. Listening is not something you do; instead, it is a way of being. Intentional listening requires that you turn down the noise in your mind and silence the internal monologue. Like meditation, it requires focusing your attention.

Intentional listening is actually an innate skill that is unlearned as our ego becomes emboldened. Mothers are hardwired to be intentional listeners. They remain focused on their children's every utterance. That intensity comes from a sense of absolute commitment. The intentional listener is able to reconnect with that commitment. When organic leaders are themselves intentional listeners and have intentional leaders in their organizations, there is a shared commitment to the organization. Commitment is a repellent to conflict. Commitment allows conversation, interaction and continuous improvement to thrive. Commitment is our intention to see other people as worthy and important as we shift attention from ourselves and onto other individuals.

At the Bama Companies we encourage everyone to listen with a purpose. This requires being aware of your internal monologue while someone else is speaking. When the internal monologue tries to assert itself, the listener must interrupt it with one question: What is the purpose of my listening right now? While the ego may have various responses, the intentional listener will remind himself or herself that the purpose is to hear and comprehend the speaker rather than evaluate what is being said.

All notions and opinions we have are learned ideas. Each person has a history, experiences, relationships and a background that influence their beliefs and responses to their environment and situations. The intentional listener is aware of that uniqueness in each of us and is able to be empathetic and responsive to ideas expressed by others.

Awareness is what allows anyone to become an intentional listener. This awareness comes from recognizing words, phrases, behaviors, gestures and intonations that distract the mind and enable the ego (these are often referred to as "hot buttons"). The intention of a conversation is not to insert righteousness; rather, it is to share knowledge. When an intentional listener becomes aware of their hot buttons, he or she can refocus their attention back on the speaker and ask themselves: "What am I supposed to learn?" This clears their mind and becomes a receptacle of the words.

The intentional listener develops the ability to concentrate. Because they have the ability to concentrate on a speaker, they can carry that skill to other aspects of the organization and are better able to concentrate on tasks. Concentration, the attention to detail and the needs of others, are directly tied to quality and improvement.

Deadlines, to-do lists, noisy equipment or crowded rooms can all get in the way of listening. The best way to concentrate in spite of distractions is to deal with them first. Putting the distractions aside allows you to give the speaker the courtesy of your undivided attention. If the distractions will not vacate your mind, then be honest with the speaker and say, "I'm distracted right now. Can we talk in an hour when I can give you my full attention?" Honesty is another show of respect to the speaker.

Intentional listening is the key to success however you and your organization define success. Distraction keeps us from performing at our best, but intentional listening builds relationships. At the Bama Companies we are aware that our jobs depend on getting cooperation from other people. Intentional listening cannot be delegated; it can only be accomplished voluntarily. The intentional listener is empowered by their sense of self-control and commitment. Anyone who feels more in charge of themselves generally is someone who feels less stressed and more content. Contented people bring positive energy to their organizations.

Intentional listening is the best investment an organization can make. Neither money nor technology are needed to make this investment, but it must be modeled by management and developed by everyone in the organization. The following techniques can help anyone become an intentional listener.

People should be encouaged to:

1. Leave your own concerns to one side. You can't focus on somebody else if you are also thinking about your problems or concerns.

2. Allow sufficient time. For example, feeling rushed to attend a meeting causes the listener to want the speaker to hurry up and finish. Their attention is on the clock, not the speaker.

3. Quell the urge to respond. Talk less, listen more.

4. Use eye contact. It is hard for a speaker to continue if the person they are addressing is not looking at them.

5. Use gestures (i.e., nod of the head) to affirm you are listening to the speaker. Encourage them to elaborate. Body language more than words lets the speaker know you are engaged.

6. Clarify and confirm what the speaker has said so they know you have heard them. This includes validating their feelings (i.e., you sound frustrated).

7. Don't pretend. If your attention has wandered, be honest. Ask the person to repeat what they have said rather than guess. Your honesty will be appreciated.

8. Be patient. Sometimes people will be muddled or verbose. You can help them to tell their story, but don't rush them at a pace too quick for them.

9. Avoid "me, too" comments or discussing how what the speaker is saying affects you. Show empathy, but don't take over the conversation.

10. Try not to become defensive; listen to what the speaker is saying and don't take it personally.

11. Don't interrupt until you are very clear what the speaker is saying. They may have some insightful thoughts that you will miss if you interrupt their train of thought.

12. Don't rush to fill the silence; give the speaker time to think. Wait a second or two before you respond.

13. Show empathy; put yourself in the speaker's shoes to gain perspective.

14. Don't rush to fix what is expressed and avoid criticism. Really think about what was said before giving advice.

15. Be aware of your hot buttons. Try and avoid being judgmental; take the time to get clarity on what is really being said.

16. Eliminate external distraction. If you are in a location which is hot, cold, noisy or uncomfortable, look to move to a different place. You can't concentrate if you are in a situation or environment that demands a lot of your attention.

17. Notice how other people make you feel when they listened to you.

Intentional listeners are enablers. Enabling is usually associated with negative behaviors, but when people feel validated and listened to they are enabled to do their best. Ability is the capacity to get things done. Treating people with enmity causes them to be resistant and resentful, but treating them with respect empowers them. Intentional listening more than performance reviews, promotions or monetary bonuses shows respect.

People are motivated by what they consider to be important to them, which is based upon their own values. When we listen to others we gain an appreciation of what the speaker needs in order to feel appreciated, secure or fulfilled. Too many organizational goals are tied to factors that have nothing to do with the needs and values of the people within the organization. Too often business leaders believe that employees can be intimidated into performing tasks to get the work done. True, the tasks may be completed, but innovation and continuous improvement will not occur. To motivate people they must be listened to and their needs understood. Research has proven that being sensitive to the needs of others produces mutual respect.[17] People who know they are being heard are willing to follow leaders into battle.

People want to know their values matter. If they sense they are not being heard, if they perceive that waste, inefficiency and insincerity are condoned, they will not feel a sense of loyalty to the organization. People want to know that their work is being done for a business or organization that doesn't cut corners, engage in favoritism or manipulate them. They want to know they are being heard, that they are being treated fairly and respected. Respect projects positive energy, which motivates employees to act within the best interest of the organization. At the Bama Companies we know that treating employees with fairness and integrity lays the foundation for motivation, meaning morale problems are rare.

Integrity and fairness are our core values. Innovation and continuous improvement occur in this positive environment.

Intentional listening cannot be feigned; it needs to be authentic. When people know you are being authentic they are willing to show mutual respect. Unchallenged agreement is not the goal. Participants in any culture will not always agree, but shared values and being valued will keep people motivated and engaged.

---

[17] Mike Vance and Diane Deacon. *Break Out of the Box*, Career Press, Franklin Lakes, New Jersey, 1996, 105.

Many situations will arise where tact and diplomacy are required; this does not negate the need for sensitivity and authenticity. People will always sense when the people they are interacting with are true to their values. Motivation and creativity thrive when managers and coworkers respond to employees' needs based on authentic values.

It is important to note that valuing and validating others is not synonymous with exempting them from standards. The organization's standards are shared values of the organization's culture. Balance is achieved when the organization's standards appreciate employees' needs for acceptance and fulfillment. People do not expect to be lulled or coddled; they are inspired and motivated by challenges and the improvements they can enact. Motivation is a result of meeting human expectations and people meeting their expectations for themselves. The only way we can know those expectations is to encourage people to express them and show willingness in what they have to say.

Intentional listening benefits both the organization and the individual listener. People who are good listeners are recognized as helpful and empathetic. They garner trust. That trust allows them to exert more influence over others than those who are not accomplished listeners. People who are authentic, intentional listeners are also listened to more by others. Intentional listeners are involved in fewer conflicts and are perceived as more positive and effective regardless of their level or rank in an organization.

Intentional listening is empowering because one of the most powerful ways to understand the self is to understand others. This is because inside of each of us is a tiny version of all of us.[18] As we come to a more intimate and complete understanding of those around us through intentional listening, we in turn come to a deeper understanding and appreciation of who we truly are and what we can accomplish.

This allows us to feel more confident in our abilities. All of our relationships in and outside the workplace are fortified by our ability to appreciate another person's point of view and why they act or respond the way they do in various situations. Understanding is the source of all knowledge, and knowledge is the key to continuous improvement.

---

[18] Ken Wallace. "8 Ways to Listen for True Understanding." Franklin Covey, http://www.teambuildingtips.com/team-building-articles/team-communication/8-ways-to-listen-for-true-understanding.html.

These improvements are possible only when employees are motivated. As discussed, those who are validated are motivated. Intentional listening is the most efficient and authentic way to validate others.

In *Out of the Crisis*, Dr. Deming wrote: "The aim of leadership should be to improve the performance of man and machine, to improve quality, to increase output and simultaneously to bring pride to the workmanship of people."[19]

---

[19] W. Edward Deming. *Out of the Crisis*, Massachusetts Institute of Technology Press, 1982, 248.

MISSION, VISION AND VALUES

Each person within the organization should be able to articulate his or her own Personal Mission Statement that can roll into the corporate Mission Statement.

An example of an organic leader's Mission Statement is:

> *My mission is to create, nurture and maintain an environment of growth, challenge and continuous improvement for all within our organization.*

If each person's own Mission Statement does not match or relate to the organization's Mission Statement, then everyone within the organization, as well as customers and suppliers, will be underserved and unhappy. Not only should all employees know the organization's Mission Statement, all managers and leaders should know the Mission Statements of the individuals in their organization. Ideally, they should all compliment each other.

The organization's Mission Statement should reflect your exceptional product or service. *The quality of Bama employees is, in essence, the formula for quality in our products and services.* At the Bama Companies, we recognize that it is only the unique contribution of our employees which ensures the superior quality of our products. Therefore, the core of our Mission Statement is, "People helping people be successful." It is surprising that most businesses and organizations do not include employees in their Mission Statements.

For too long, corporations have treated Mission Statements as nothing more than platitudes or pleasantries to be posted on wall plaques. But this cynicism has allowed Western business culture and many companies to go awry. What employees, suppliers and consumers have come to realize is that corporate management, MBA programs and Human Resource Departments have been saying one thing and doing another. Their empty Mission Statements, which lack sincerity, have not served them and have not been able to bolster their organizations' needs in times of stress.

A Mission Statement should be no more than one sentence in length, easily understood and memorable. Corporations hold costly retreats and spend tens of thousands of dollars on consultants to develop what should come organically from the organization.

> *WE ARE CONTINUOUSLY IMPROVING OUR PRACTICES SO THAT WE MAY INCREASE IN SIZE AND SERVE INNOVATIVE NEW PRODUCTS TO OUR MARKET. AS IT EXPANDS ITS MARKETS AND PRODUCT LINES, BAMA WILL OFFER TO EACH STAKEHOLDER SIGNIFICANT OPPORTUNITY TO GROW, TO INCREASE THEIR PERSONAL WEALTH AND TO BE PART OF A PACESETTING COMPANY.*

Organizations and companies are made up of individuals, each with their own mission, vision and values. Your operation must be a melding of the individuals into each other with each participant realizing that the mission is always larger than a job. This requires contemplation and reflection, skills that are too easily lost in a society obsessed with technology and quick action. Neither individuals nor organizations can define their mission until they know themselves. What we think about ourselves is explicitly reflected in what we say or do. Therefore, it is important to honestly evaluate who we really are to our coworkers, customers, suppliers and community. Do others comprehend us in the way we perceive ourselves? If not, we must understand why and either redefine our mission or modify our operations to fit our mission.

This requires focus. The mission statement should be broad enough to allow for the diversity (new products, new services and new markets) required of your operation, but specific enough to be meaningful. Most importantly, it must convey a purpose. All activities within the organization should flow from and relate back to the organization's Mission Statement.

By crafting a clear Mission Statement, you can powerfully communicate your intentions and motivate your business or organization to realize an attractive and inspiring common vision of the future as they learn from the past and operate in the present. A good Mission Statement is inspiring, exciting, clear and engaging.

While a Mission Statement encompasses what needs to be done in the present, the Vision Statement is about sustaining the mission into the future. The ability of employees to see what is possible beyond the present moment allows them to be creative and innovative. At the Bama Companies, we believe it is imperative that we are clear about what we are creating and compare it to what we intend to create. This is the path of continuous improvement.

The Vision Statement communicates both the purpose and values of the organization. It inspires employees and suppliers to give their best, and gives customers confidence as to why they should continue to work with the organization.

Too often businesses and organizations create a Mission Statement and goals and objectives but do not articulate their vision. To create a Vision Statement:

1. Draw on the beliefs, mission and environment of the organization.

2. Describe what you want to achieve in the future.

3. Be specific to each area within the organization.

4. Be positive and inspiring and encourage creativity.

5. Do not assume that the organization will have the same framework as it does today.

6. Be open to change throughout the organization.

The Vision Statement must encompass the shared beliefs of the organization and is a public and visible statement of it. These shared beliefs guide the actions of everyone involved: employees, suppliers, customers and the community. They reflect the knowledge, philosophy and intended actions of the organization.

The Bama Companies' Vision Statement is:

CREATE AND DELIVER LOYALTY, PROSPERITY AND FUN WHILE CONTINUOUSLY IMPROVING OUR PRODUCTS AND SERVICES.

A compelling Vision Statement can help guide the organization through difficult and challenging times if it is embedded with positive expectations. A Vision Statement is beneficial to the organization because it recognizes the operation has an ongoing purpose.

Other benefits include:

1. Encouraging employees, suppliers and customers to think beyond traditional ways of thinking.

2. Providing continuity and avoids resistance to new ideas.

3. Promoting ongoing interest and commitment.

4. Encouraging openness to unique and creative solutions.

5. Encouraging and building confidence.

6. Building loyalty through involvement and sense of ownership.

7. Allows us to keep moving forward and envision the future.

Vision allows the organization to move beyond the factors that often hold it back such as fear, tradition, complacency, short-term goals, stereotypes and naysayers. A Vision Statement rejects the negative by focusing on what is possible, the picture of the future you and your organization want to create. An effective Vision Statement will therefore tell the world what change you wish to create for the future of your organization and the people and community it serves.

A Vision Statement ultimately defines the organization's purpose in terms of the organization's values, rather than bottom-line measures, since values are guiding beliefs about how things should be done. The Vision Statement communicates both the purpose and values of the organization. For employees, it gives direction about how they are expected to contribute and inspires them to give their best. Shared with customers, it shapes customers' understanding of why they should continue to work with the organization or business.

A compelling vision, when stated clearly and positively, has the ability to pull positive employees and committed suppliers and customers to the organization or business, making it a powerful business tool. RememberConce the Vision Statement is formulated, it is important to keep it in the collective consciousness of the organization's mind by continually reminding everyone of what is possible.

The organic leader must then move beyond the written word and connect with the heart and purpose of each person who shows up to work every day, each one bringing with them their own values and beliefs.

This is where, I believe, American and Western corporations have strayed the farthest. When Human Resource managers, C-suite executives and board compensation committee members sit down to discuss how everyone in the company is to be paid, quite often any thought of value to the company goes right out the window. Our culture has allowed the desire to make money to overshadow and contaminate the essence of our being. Employees, their values, their purpose and their beliefs all take a backseat to the importance of the top officers' seven figure salary discussions.

We can cleanse our organizations and create healthy operations if we work from a base of shared values and overhaul our ineffective executive compensation systems. Instead of incentivizing individual firefighting and short-term thinking, why not incent people to work together?

What if management's job was to keep the company in business for twenty-five, fifty or one hundred years!! I can assure you, the decisions would be dramatically different if they were managing for three generations from now, instead of next quarter's profit. Building a company slowly from a continuous improvement point of view would dramatically change the landscape of American business. When did everything in a business have to operate at WARP speed? When our public company executives needed double digit stock price growth in three to five years, or lose their stock options and bonus money.

Both the Mission Statement and Vision Statement are reflections of an organization's values. An organization's values influence everything about the operation and exhibit what the leaders and managers really care about, such as the differentiation between quality and product. As Roy O. Disney, chairman of Disneyland, stated, "We manage by our values because decision-making is easy when you know what your values are."[20]

Values are the standards we consider important enough to act upon. They influence our behavior and the behavior of

---

[20] Mike Vance and Diane Deacon. *Break Out of the Box,* Career Press, Franklin Lakes, New Jersey, 1996, 102.

others. Even through challenging times in an organization, it is the shared, practiced values that keep people feeling fulfilled and purpose-driven.

Positive values support a healthy environment that fosters creativity and continuous improvement. Creativity and innovation, as well as ensuring organizational success, improve the quality of life of others. Valuing innovation and creativity allows people to seek a better way and a greater truth.

Values are the principles by which we decide what our standards are, what our behaviors are and how we are going to live. Our values guide our life choices, our intended code of conduct. Organic leaders know that expressing values and acting according to those stated values influence others in a positive way. Values cannot just be stated or imposed; commitment only comes from being authentic and acting and living by them. For example, a stated value might be to treat coworkers and employees as partners in the organization. But if every idea that is presented is rejected, then the value is not valid because it is not reflected in action.

One way to blend value and action is to remember that the more individual values and organizational objectives are linked, the better chance for innovation and continuous improvement.

People draw upon the values of their family, culture, peer group, religious affiliation and other associations, and they bring those personal values into the workplace. Knowing those values and giving people the opportunity to be guided by them in the workplace garners commitment. More importantly, workers who can come up with new ways to apply their constructive values are more likely to come up with solutions to challenges.

Too often the only value expressed in a business is the financial result. This is not a constructive value and impedes progress. Instead, an organization's values should truly reflect its practices and they must be authentic. Just stating a value is not enough to instill it into the organization's culture. If you profess a value but do not follow it, commitment wanes and people become cynical. Values must be enacted in the process and performance of everyone in the organization.

You can't just say you "care for your people"; that care and commitment must be enacted, perceived and felt by everyone in the organization. This may mean that managers spend less time in closed-door meetings and more time interacting with people one-on-one.

Demonstrating values is time-consuming, is not a quick fix and requires a consciousness of your actions compared to your words, but adhering to them is the best way to ensure the organization's mission and vision.

Values are important to leaders and managers in two ways. If you are working with others, you must be able to appeal to the mutually accepted and understood values, and when working independently, it is the adherence to those values that keeps you on track. Leadership without values is not really leadership. To be effective, the organic leader must operate by the professed values. If the values are vague or hard to understand and not modeled, the organization will slip into cynicism and apathy.

Your values must be consistent and easy to express. Write them down and refer to them often. Compare your understanding of the organization's values with others to reinforce that they are shared. When everyone understands and accepts the organization's values, they remain motivated and committed to the organization's vision.

Shared values help minimize individual egos because everyone knows and has bought into the shared values. They understand that it is not one person's will or idea that is being enforced but the commitment to the shared values that matter. People are less defensive when they know that everyone is operating under the same values and that those values are authentic and upheld by everyone in the organization.

This minimizes the need to enforce rules. Rules limit creativity and foster resistance whereas shared values provide personal responsibility for everyone. Successful companies are the ones who have employees with entrepreneurial spirits and are focused on results and improvements rather than rules.

They are fulfilled by living up to commitments rather than looking for ways to "bend the rules." Clearly defined values are the cornerstone of personnel accountability.

Leaders must remain cognizant that values only work it they are accepted and enacted by everyone. This includes the highest ranking officials in any organization. If a value is not being upheld, it may be time to evaluate it to see if it is still relevant or needs to be revised. Reacting intelligently to a challenge by assessing the stated value is not compromising your own values; it is being responsible to the shared vision of the organization. How many times in the last two years have you found yourself saying, "I can't believe CEOs do THAT" after watching the evening news?

When people know you are willing to adjust to challenges and circumstances, they know they are empowered to be creative and innovative. This means they are open and not afraid to fail. Those who are empowered to try are motivated to find solutions. Values are aspired to while rules must be followed. If people are given the chance to live up to the organization's shared values, they will be motivated to succeed rather than scared not to fail. Innovation and creativity, and the positive results that accompany them, result from authentic, shared values.

There are five basic values that most people share and should be a part of organizations and businesses:

1. People expect that life will be just and that they will be treated with integrity. Integrity produces fairness because it adheres to a principle of positive values.

2. People expect authenticity. People shut down when actions don't match words. For people to remain motivated, there must be an authentic response to needs based on shared, practiced values.

3. People expect that they will experience acceptance and understanding. Accepting and understanding people's individuality does not mean holding them to different standards; rather, they feel supported as they try and live by the shared values. Organic leaders are able to be empathetic to individual needs and acceptance while instilling in employees a commitment to the organization's shared values.

4. People expect to interact with others who are rational and respectful. They want to work with people who are rational rather than adversarial. Rational relationships often turn into long-term commitments while adversarial relationships tend to create conflict, which is unproductive. Rational relationships are about shared vision, productivity and continuous improvement.

5. Solve problems because that gives purpose to their lives. Instead of trying to control employees, give them opportunities to overcome challenges and achieve. Encourage people to take chances.

People expect that life will be fulfilling. For many people, the prospect of a new day is invigorating. So when the workplace is dull and unimaginative, they become unmotivated.

The quest for fulfillment and stimulation is an ingrained human desire.

People want to meet challenges.

People who are motivated believe they can accomplish anything. Self-motivated people are responsible for most of the world's products and services. They are positive problem solvers who value action over mere words.

Through Bama's focus on people, they in turn, will focus a culture of care and concern on their families, themselves and their communities.

People in our organization share these values and are committed to maintaining them. Our mission, vision and values resonate through each and every person who works in our organization. We all come to Bama for different reasons, but we stay because of our shared mission, vision and values.

> *The Bama brand; a brand that stands for quality, safety, taste, value and honesty ... Our brand is respected worldwide.*

CHAPTER EIGHT
THE PURSUIT OF PERFECTION

Learning exists from the day we are born until the day we die. Nothing is ever the same moment to moment, day to day, quarter to quarter or year to year. People are not robots; their minds need stimulation. How can businesses operate unless real, feeling people show up to work? Too many organizations are filled with people who don't really care to be there. They are untrained, unmotivated people spending time talking to their friends and coworkers instead of helping customers. Conversely, we as customers find companies who serve us with a smile and systems that work to mutual benefit. We are so ecstatic, we become brand loyalists, telling everyone we meet what a great company really looks like.

The Bama Companies sponsor programs that allow employees to proactively seek opportunities, take action and pursue ideas and challenges that solve problems for customers and consumers. We also encourage all employees to seek a college education by providing tuition reimbursement

By encouraging lifelong learning, skill training and product and process development, employees are motivated to find new and better ways to do their jobs and respond to internal and external customer needs. One such example is what I call our innovation center. The Marshall Tech Center, a key tool in our product development process, helps us put our words into action.

As stated in chapter 7, words written, spoken or both, in America's and Western corporations are woefully missing the mark. Customer service (internal and external) no longer seems to be a priority in Western business. The previous chapter focused on formulating meaningful words and expressing them verbally and on paper. The words are important, but words alone are not enough. Employees need an entire arsenal of tools.

Proficiency means employees have obtained the knowledge and developed the skill to do their jobs with confidence. This confidence and pride mean that not only do they have ability, but are willing to move their expertise forward in the pursuit of perfection or what we at the Bama Companies call "Continuous Improvement."

When people are proficient and confident, their knowledge and work ethic are appreciated by others and they set the standard for everyone in the organization. What we have come to understand is that this is not about attaining a specific goal or crossing a proverbial finish line. It means continuing to move further to continue to pursue excellence and lift everyone toward greater value and purpose. Excellence is not static; there is always something that can be made better, always something new to be learned.

The misnomer is that for people to be proficient and to rise to the top of their profession, they must be driven. It has been my experience that inspiration is more enduring than drive and that balance is what allows people to pursue excellence over a long period of time rather than getting burned out by always feeling driven.

We want all of our employees to have a sense of balance, which means promoting not only their financial pursuits, but their physical, intellectual, spiritual and psychological well-being, too. The appreciation of proficiency and balance not only results in a better workforce, it allows everyone within the organization to be the best people they can be for their families, community, society and themselves.

People who are well physically have the best chance of being well emotionally and thus able to focus on their work. We want all of our employees to obtain and maintain the best possible physical condition throughout the stages of their lives. In 2007, Bama opened a Bama Family Medical Clinic that is free to all employees and their families. The clinic has a doctor and a chiropractor on staff. We have introduced smoking cessation programs and reduced the amount of junk food in our vending machines.

Learning is not only obtained through traditional means. Through experience, the learner gains knowledge. Information is static, but knowledge is dynamic and continues to live within us. Wisdom is the ultimate level of understanding and as with knowledge, it operates within us. Peter Drucker said it best: "Knowledge is information that changes something or somebodyCeither by becoming grounds for actions, or by making an individual (or an institution) capable of different or more effective action."[21]

Spiritual well-being is not about supporting (or suppressing) religion. For us, it has to do with the belief that we are part of a meaningful universe. What we do as individuals and as an organization has purpose and value. This belief gives us a sense of connection; we are part of an organization, a community, a culture, a universe. This means we foster caring, charity and concern. This is based on Stephen Covey's Principle-Centered Organization. He teaches that when you center your organization on correct principles, it is not easily threatened by external circumstances and even competition becomes a healthy learning source.

Covey's Four Key Principles (trustworthiness, trust, empowerment and alignment) require each of us to align our lives, progressively, with the core principles from the inside out.[22]

---

[21] Peter Drucker. *New Realities,* Google Books, 91.

[22] Stephen R. Covey. *Principle-Centered Leadership,* Fireside Press, New York, 1992, 60-64.

1. Personal: your relationship with yourself.

2. Interpersonal: your relationships and interactions with others.

3. Managerial: your responsibility to get your job done.

4. Organizational: your need to organize people (recruit, train, compensate, team-building, problem-solving, alignment, etc.).

Internally we support spiritual well-being through our standard of ethical behavior specified in our prime directives. These guidelines transcend time or circumstance and include establishing behavioral norms where violation is intolerable and illuminate the essence of the organization, its mythology and its defining concepts. Specifically they are:

1. Bama is in the business to generate revenue, have fun and make stakeholders successful.

2. Bama treats all people (employees, suppliers, customers, consumers) with respect and dignity.

3. The quality and safety of Bama's products will not be compromised under any circumstances.

4. Bama respects the community, the culture and the planet.

Externally, Bama strengthens its immediate community (Tulsa, Oklahoma) and the surrounding area with the spirit of giving that has far-reaching implications. Financial contributions, employee volunteer hours and product donations are all contributing factors to the company's cultural beliefs.

An organization or business is only as strong as the individuals who comprise it. This means encouraging people to like and accept themselves. It means being comfortable with who you are and maintaining a healthy sense of self-esteem. This is made difficult in the workplace because people often get mired in guilt. This does not mean people should not be held accountable for their actions or outcomes, but should understand the root cause and be encouraged and motivated to learn from challenges and circumstances and move beyond them. Self-acceptance is the key to psychological well-being. This means individuals can see situations in perspective and are willing to be flexible.

By focusing on the physical, intellectual, spiritual and physiological well-being of the organization and the people who comprise it, the financial well-being of both will prevail. Because money is not the measure of well-being but the outcome of it, people are given the opportunity to live harmonious, balanced lives. Proficiency in the core principle areas gives people perspective about money so that instead of it controlling them, they control it.

While organizations have an obligation to work with existing staff, injecting positive people and energy into the company must be part of the recruiting process. Perhaps personnel and Human Resource Departments ask the wrong questions in interviews. If we asked candidates…:

1. How do you view life?

2. What have been your critical experiences in life?

3. What are the moral values that guide you?

4. How do you feel people should be managed?

5. What do you consider beautiful?

. . . instead of the standard questions, businesses and organizations would have a better chance of creating a balanced, harmonious workplace.

Perceptive managers and leaders know their personnel and who is committed to proficiency and well-being by observing not only actions, but their attitudes. Those striving for excellence and continuous improvement are willing to do a task, no matter how menial, again and again, until they get it right. Every job, big or small, is handled with the same level of care and attention.

The self-motivated person is not obsessed with the goal or target; they are confident enough to know the objective will be obtained. Instead, their focus is on what needs to be done to reach the goal. They master time; time does not control them. Proficiency comes with execution and measured patience.

The proficient person has the tools required to get the job done. It is the organization's responsibility to supply the tools and train the workforce to use them. It is the responsibility of the employee to master the tools and to let management know when they do not have the tools they need to succeed.

The self-motivated, proficient person is empowered, because they have a sense of well-being, are well trained and know they can execute any task. They are willing to go beyond their job description and see a problem all the way through to its appropriate solution.

There are not shortcuts to proficiency or perfection. The path to perfection is to be patient enough to keep trying. Attention to detail is a must combined with the understanding that there are not menial tasks. Those pursuing excellence see challenges as transforming and as an opportunity to progress from one phase of their career to another.

Along with patience, attention to detail, the proper tools and a sense of well-being, in order for organizations to continually pursue perfection they must foster an environment of mutual respect. Organizations cannot expect people to feel empowered if they are not respected. Self-respect is actually the origin of mutual respect. If you grant yourself the respect you deserve, you'll attain the same respect among others. Developing and maintaining self-respect as the pursuit of perfection is an ongoing process. Respect, as in every other aspect of the organization's growth, requires continuous attention to it. This is vital since it is only through mutual respect that relationships can grow and the dedication to continuous improvement can thrive.

Real mutual respect develops only when one individual can identify fully with another. By sharing fully in the experiences of others and being willing to involve yourself with their experiences, instead of staying only within your own interests, it allows you to develop a mutually accepting way of relating to others. Every member of the organization, regardless of their task or level, has something important to contribute. The organic leader cultivates fairness among people at all levels to ensure that integrity remains in place not only when facing challenges but in everyday matters. At the Bama Companies, we have discovered that when you give anyone in the organization the opportunity to help solve problems and participate in solutions, they become so highly motivated that they will continue looking for improvements in other areas. Our creed is to uphold and honor those who are successful and encourage others to ask questions and share ideas.

Business people must be willing to give up their reliance on numbers only, and begin to open up their intuitive gifts, to open their hearts, and really connect with the people with whom they work. We must use business as a tool to help engage our souls at every level. We cannot be afraid of being humiliated, nor will we be intimidated into changing our desires. We all must demand to be treated better, and to be allowed to bring our souls to work with us, and be engaged in organizations that help the world improve itself.

> CONTINUOUS IMPROVEMENT IS NOT A COMPANY POLICY—IT IS A LIFESTYLE.

Bama's CFO Bill Chew

Continuous improvement requires constant adaptation by obtaining and using information and by evaluating changes to make sure what is implemented is effective. It requires reliable information about your environment from a variety of sources who evaluate your outcomes (what you do) and your processes (how you do it).

The ability to pull people together from different levels and areas to freely discuss the information and issues involved is also a crucial element of an organic leader. Participants must be encouraged to come up with ideas, evaluate them, choose some and carry them out. Then there must be a systematic way to measure progress and the outcomes of changes.

Most of all, the collective consciousness of the organization must have a real desire to make things happen, even if it means relinquishing power, changing relationships and doing some things you do not completely agree with at the time.

The initial focus on continuous improvement must be gathering information. Unfortunately, too many people routinely get and ignore feedback. By making use of feedback mandatory, the company avoids alienating customers and wasting time. Getting information and not using it lowers trust, increases frustration and costs money. Information leads to knowledge and knowledge leads to wisdom. It is through wisdom and consciousness that the never-ending pursuit of excellence resides.

Continuous improvement cannot be run only at the top, or even just at management levels. The employees are the ones who continually gather information at every level of the business or organization's operation. Using their ideas is vital to continuous improvement; the most successful programs seem to be the ones that have the highest staff involvement, regardless of task level.

Another aspect of continuous improvement is developing useful measurements and using them consistently. They should be used as a basis to work with other people. Measurement instills in employees the organization's value of continuing to strive for improvement, and not waiting for new technology, people or management to make changes.

People can tell when they are doing things right, and that pride keeps them in a personal, continuous improvement cycle. Continuous improvement requires dedication and a willingness to be guided by objective information sources and the priorities of the organization. We still set our goals and choose where we want to go, but our job becomes easier because change becomes easier, and that means we have more resources. Continuous improvement makes working fun because it encourages experimentation and controlled risk. This brings a level of excitement to the environment and motivates people to work together towards common goals. With shared information and a sense of purpose, businesses and organizations become nicer places to work.

The results of sustained, serious and continuous improvement programs speak for themselves. With a little effort and a lot of dedication, practicing continuous improvement becomes more than just a phrase.

I believe now, more than ever, that America and Western corporate culture is in need of an overhaul of its management practices. The processes described in this book are the first of a multi-step process, a process that is necessary in order to proceed down the path of a new American (Western) corporate and business profile.

CHAPTER NINE
THE LAW OF INDUCTIVE REASONING

Since 1927, my grandmother encouraged us all to look for ways to get better every day. My father was consumed by doing something new so often, he drove us all crazy with new product ideas and new pieces of equipment he would pick up at auctions all over the country. My mom was always the voice of reason; she kept him in line with facts. Facts like, "Paul, we just don't have the money for all of these new things!"

She was right; most people can't assimilate change so fast. Staying the course, focusing on what you do well and repeating this day in and day out help organizations become extremely proficient in production, safety and quality, engineering, marketing and sales.

I would say our culture at the Bama Companies is a direct reflection of my mom and dad's values. We encourage our team members to look for opportunities to improve things. This has always been the way of our family. "Improvement, take it one day at a time," my dad used to say. Today, we talk about engagement and innovation. During the 1930s, my parents asked their employees to help them make the company a success.

My parents were involved ... they walked the floor; they worked side-by-side with our employees. My father would take food to their homes if they were sick, and come back to let my mom know he wanted to raise the wages. He was concerned that they weren't improving their lives fast enough. My dad was an owner who asked for help, worked alongside people and visited them at their homes. Each employee helped develop a culture of caring and family values, making Bama more than just a business.

One of the things my family never had much tolerance for was complaining. I remember on the way to school one morning I was complaining how Dad made us get up early to go see our new production line. I accompanied him begrudgingly.

I was such a little snot, I didn't smile at anyone, and I wasn't friendly to any of the plant workers. When we were finished walking around, Dad told me to go into his office. He handed me pictures of some of the homes where the ladies on the production line lived. He asked me if I realized how lucky I was and said he never wanted me to act like that again!

I was a changed girl after that. I realized how much complaining I did, and I also realized that complaining did nothing to improve things. Often, it takes us a while to realize that our complaining leads to nowhere, and actually, energetically makes things worse.

> IT IS WITHIN THE POWER OF EVERY PERSON TO IMAGINE AND IMPLEMENT CHANGE.

What I learned after I met my mentor, Dr. Deming, is that people are not motivated by money. Money is a tool that allows people to function in our world, but it is not the lifeblood of human existence. Life is dependent upon stimulation and movement. As babies, we are born with natural curiosity.

Being inquisitive is internal stimulation of the mind ... it is the product of a mind that's alive and awake.

What distinguishes human beings from other living beings is that our minds require movement, and in addition, progression and solving problems. We also desire to understand how things work. Continuous improvement is hardwired in the human psyche, until our fear of humiliation takes over and forces us into a dark closet. Fear of being humiliated in front of others is the number one fear a human being has. The other gripping fear of all humans is being left alone. Either of these fears is always at the base of our actions. When a person really begins to understand how many of the actions they take in life are to avoid being left alone, or being humiliated in front of others, they have begun a journey to the place Buddha calls "self-enlightenment."

> IT TAKES **COURAGE AND PERSONAL DESIRE** TO CHANGE TO CONTINUOUSLY IMPROVE YOUR LIFE.

Since companies are made up by large groups of people who are all afraid of being left alone (fired) or humiliated (reprimanded and possibly fired), it is hard for companies to encourage personal growth. CEOs who have no time for real learning and real improvement push people past their own personal competencies. When things don't improve quickly enough, managers often lose faith in their team members. It is then they turn to one of the most dreaded strategies known by people around the world ... THE DREADED CONSULTING FIRM.

So many companies and organizations depend upon consultants, MBAs and advisors to determine how to run their operations. No academic or managerial theory has the power or promise of the Law of Inductive Reasoning.

Throughout the United States and Western world of the twentieth century we have seen monumental growth in material gain. We now know that material gain is void of purpose if mental and spiritual prowess is not part of all of our interactions. This is not merely New Age thought; this is a scientific reality. Science, particularly in the realm of quantum physics, has allowed for innovation and progress in a variety of fields from electronics to medicine. The basis for any advancement is energy. Physical science has resolved matter into molecules, molecules into atoms and atoms into energy. As Sir Ambrose Fleming said, "In its ultimate essence, energy may be incomprehensible to us except as an exhibition of the direct operation of that which we call mind or will." Early proponents of induction, such as Francis Bacon, saw it as a way of understanding nature in an unbiased way, as it derives laws from neutral observation.

Scientists and philosophers such as Albert Einstein knew that the most powerful forces in nature are the "invisible" forces. There is nothing tangible about a mathematical formula, but whether we are landing a man on the moon or constructing a house, it is those intangible calculations that allow us to invent and produce. For humankind, the most powerful forces are also "invisible" ones.

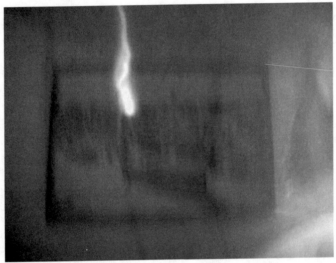

The only way a person can create, produce and live is through touching their own heart with love and compassion for themselves first, and ultimately that love flows out to others. Thoughts, brought about by silence and meditation, is the only activity that the human spirit possesses, and thought is the only product of the activity of thinking.

Because addition and subtraction are invisible, they can be considered spiritual in nature. Reasoning, too, is a spiritual process. Ideas are nothing more than spiritual notions, which lead to action.

Ideas are not conjecture or ethereal; they are connected to and a product of the physical tissues and neurons of the brain.

Conscience-focused thoughts produce a physical change in the construction of brain tissue. Therefore, a certain number of thoughts on any given subject is capable of bringing about significant change.

Not only are ideas a vehicle for change, but how ideas and thoughts are perceived is the determining factor on whether we will take action. Thoughts of courage, power, inspiration and harmony are positive and when allowed to replace failure, despair, limitation and discord (which are negative) improvement will prevail. Again, this is not theoretical; scientific study has shown that thoughts actually take root in brain tissue. When people see situations in a positive light, old ideas will be laid to rest and new ideas will flourish.

When individuals are given opportunities for success, possibilities are accepted as the norm. Thoughts of success are contagious. Those who are positive radiate their positivism to others. The initiator of the positive idea attracts others to a positive place in the organization. Multiple people with positive ideas and energy create a positive work environment. The simple exercise of thought is the genesis of improvement not only in the individual but in the organization and its circumstances and conditions.

The inspired leader knows that positive thoughts are the passage to continuous improvement. Those thoughts and feelings have power to enlighten. Within creative thought is the solution for every problem.

Dr. Deming called this phenomena, "Cause and Effect." A positive environment is imbued with harmony and balance, which allows health and success to flourish. What each person in the organization needs to understand is that they have the ability to control thought and how any set of circumstances will affect them.

The reality is that those who embrace life with courage, hope, enthusiasm, confidence and trust possess the tools needed to affect change and continuous improvement. When the mind thinks positively and sends these thoughts through the cerebral-spinal nervous system, a person is in balance, alive and excited about life.

Anyone who develops a thorough understanding of the law of inductive reasoning is able to control their thought process and apply this reasoning to any set of circumstances or conditions. Clear thinking and moral insight are of incalculable value to any organization. Thought is energy and positive thought is positive energy. Thought concentrated on a specific purpose leads to continuous improvement and ultimately success.

Everyone within an organization must be trained and encouraged to develop their own inner voices and sensibilities. The keener a person's sensibilities and connectivity to their own feelings, the more acute their judgment and the more knowledge they attain.

We all have the ability to be closer to our five senses, but because we have become addicted to urgency and running away from feelings, we are often out of tune with them. We use gadgets and technology to tune out because no one can hurt us that way. In this way you "lose your feelings."

Getting in touch with your feelings is not a "New Age" term. Meditative higher states lead to inductive reasoning, and should be applied to specific situations to determine synergy. As Stephen Covey says in *The 7 Habits of Highly Effective People*, "Synergy is the product of two people inclusively listening, then brainstorming multiple 'right' answers."[23] In the end, all parties feel valued and important.

To open the culture up to more powerful interactions in your organization, encourage employees to do the following:

1. Observe what is happening around them: to collect facts without bias.

2. Analysis: classify the facts, identifying patterns of regularity.

3. Inference: from the patterns, infer generalizations about the relations between the facts.

4. Confirmation: test the inference through further observation.

5. Give a plausible explanation for why it has happened providing lots of details.

---

[23] Stephen Covey. *The 7 Habits of Highly Effective People*, 265.

6. Facts, without biased management direction, anchor situations in reality, involve everyone in discussions and don't presume answers are known.

- IT IS EASIER TO GET BUY-IN IF YOU OFFER SENSORY DATA (WHAT CAN BE SEEN AND TOUCHED) BEFORE GOING INTO THE BIG PICTURE OF IDEAS AND PRINCIPLES.

- STARTING SMALL AND BUILDING UP TO THE BIG IDEAS IS LESS THREATENING THAN STARTING WITH THE BIG CONCEPTS.

Scientists develop theories, and then build experiments to either prove or disprove those theories. Newton and Descartes taught us how to systematically build theories and verify them.

Laws and theories are gained by observing what's going on around you. What if we were all as interested in our surroundings and we observed what was really going on? What if we all did our own experiments and developed our own theories?

Good scientific laws are highly generalized and may be applied in many situations to explain other phenomena. For example, the law of gravity was used to understand why our world works the way it does. What keeps us sticking to the ground? What keeps things from flying all around us all the

time? When was the last time you thought about how things really work?

When presenting a situation, show the cause and effect that is in operation. Help the other person see why things have happened or will happen as they do. Show purpose and link things to higher values. Show the inevitable linkage between what happens first and what happens next. Go beyond correlation (that may show coincidence) and give irrefutable evidence of causality.

Human beings have a deep need for explanation and to be able to predict what will happen. We also need to be able to appear rational to others and that they appear rational to us. When a person explains cause and effect, we are reassured that they are, indeed, reasonable people, and we will trust them. Building trust is key to fostering a continually improved environment.

Continuous improvement should be the objective of any organization's operations. Improvements in business processes translate directly to increased profits by simultaneously cutting costs and increasing marketability. Deming proved that in many cases business process improvements could have accelerating cumulative effects on the company's profits.

The reality is that most organizations have a limited amount of money to spend on business process improvement and that budget has to compete with many other priorities within the organization. In many companies, if the Operations and Human Resource Departments had their choice, they would put in new hardware, software applications; hire better "qualified" people; provide them with more training; and have an attractive working environment. However, practical considerations always force companies to pick and choose the monies they can spend on the right priorities.

But just what are the right priorities? How do you know that the training course on people skills is actually making a difference in customer satisfaction? How do you know that the expensive computer system you are considering to acquire is going to make any difference? How do you know which project to do first? As well as the law of inductive reasoning described earlier in this chapter, Pareto analysis, supported by cause and effect diagramming, is a necessary tool for decision making within organizations.

A combination of process modeling with cause and effect analysis, combined with careful design of experiments (DOE), can help a company decide how and where they can maximize their resources. In the course of operations, most companies perform design of experiments informally without realizing it, since no operation is static and adjustments are constantly being made to meet daily needs. At the Bama Companies, we realize that the combination of cause and effect analysis, Pareto charting and design of experiments help employees realize a systematic and scientific approach to doing the same things they are already doing informally.

Cause-and-effect analysis is a systematic way of generating and sorting hypotheses about possible causes of a problem. Once the root causes of problems are identified, they can be addressed rather than just focusing on the symptoms; then a DOE can be developed. A DOE is a structured, organized method for determining the relationship between factors affecting a process and the output of that process. The output of the process is the dependent variable that depends upon the independent variables, which determine outcomes.

The analysis includes:

1. Methods: the processes and procedures used to deliver products and services, which include assignment, workflow and escalation.

2. Materials: the tools, products, training, process and metrics needed to provide products and services.

3. Work Environment: the incentive, reward and appreciation structures for the employees.

4. Workforce: the purpose, knowledge, problem solving skills and commitment of the employees.

In a Deming oriented organization, teams are taught easy-to-understand problem-solving tools. People feel valued because management takes the time to talk to them, interact and ask about their families and their interests.

When powerful emotional connections are made, problem solving becomes easier. The more difficult technical tasks will be learned faster and quicker. People who are treated with respect and dignity will use the problem-solving tools provided to them with confidence. By using the tools more often, continuous improvement becomes contagious.

Cause and effect analysis, when combined with design of experiments, provides a forceful combination for business process improvement. Once put into practice, it is easy to see how the diverse factors become qualitatively related to the business process performance your organization is trying to improve.

Pareto charting allows executives a systematic way of determining how capital resources will be allocated. The top two bars of a Pareto chart suggest to management where they could apply resources to reduce problems by 80 percent. The way a Pareto anaylsis works, the first two bars represent the old 80/20 rule ... 80 percent of problems are caused by 20 percent of the issues.

When it comes to measuring the precise correlation between any one factor and the process performance, your organization needs cause and effect analysis to catalog the independent variables that you are trying to "tweak." In addition to the tools, it is in the organization's best interest to include various team members who can contribute with process knowledge. It is management's role to invite stakeholders with process knowledge into meetings, make them comfortable and open all discussion to them. They have more answers than management does because they do the jobs day in and day out!!

Too often, management believes they have all the expertise and answers. They believe it is their job to have the answers. They become afraid when they don't have the answers. When problem solving, it doesn't pay to be arrogant, especially when the company is doing poorly. The people who work in our factories, offices and service desks know what's wrong. They know and they want to help. Frequently, management turns people off and turns them away when they don't even ask them their opinion. In the top-down hierarchical structures of corporate America, the high salaried individuals toss quarters and hope the decisions they have made will make a difference. However, like any coin toss, they have a 50/50 chance of being right.

These strategies aren't about management being right or looking good. There is enough of that to go around. These strategies are proven business tools that are used very rarely in America. Most managers are only concerned about their bonuses or saving face at all costs. These strategies are about satisfying customers day in and day out. They are about building "Brand Trust" with consumers, one management decision at a time.

The DOE process will help you to identify all the factors that are linked closely with customer wants. Processes can't deliver the correct products unless the aim of the process is to satisfy the customer. In Bama, as in many corporations in America, customers exist not only externally to the organization but internally as well.

Design of experiments (DOE) provides a sane, data-directed approach to business process improvement. This systematic approach, combined with intuitive understanding, is the tool to successful operations within an organization.

Inductive reasoning is that in which we extrapolate from experience to further conclusions about what will happen. The assumption behind inductive reasoning is that known cases can provide information about unknown cases.[24]

Human beings rely on inductive reasoning all of the time. For example, we assume that the gas pedals in our cars will trigger a process that moves our car forward and that the brake pedals will stop our cars from moving. The prediction of how our car works doesn't come from all of us being mechanics; it is based upon past experiences and meeting expectation. When our car doesn't respond as expected, reason tells us that a modification to have it operate properly needs to be made. Human beings use past experiences as information on how to respond to various situations in the workplace and in life. When the law

---

[24] Trudy Govier. *Practical Study of Argument*, 289.

of inductive reasoning is applied using positive energy, the path to continuous improvement is accessible.

Of all of the applications of inductive reasoning, informal cause and effect inductive reasoning is the most prevalent and influential in our everyday lives. It is relatable to people, more so than arbitrary performance reviews based on how bonuses will be divided or competition between departments that reduce employees to mere numbers. But the most important benefit to the organization is to maintain direct involvement of team members, who sit with management and discuss causes of problems, not to complain endlessly, but to share with each other how one functional area could be, without them realizing it, causing problems for other areas.

The cause-and-effect process also takes away the need to blame something or someone for errors. In most cases, errors are caused by lack of training or communication breakdowns. By developing cultures of "solving problems without shooting messengers," people are free to measure, and then report gaps in processes.

When fear is present, problems can go on for years without being solved. It takes courage to bring problems forward. If no one ever comes forward, then fear prevails. Fear is a terrible thing in a business, but inherent to it.

My dear friend and mentor, Dusty Staub, authored two books dealing with courage in the business world. He maintains fear is the number one issue facing most companies. Dr.

Deming believed this too. When people are too afraid of being humiliated or "cut from the herd" (fear of being alone), bad things happen. In personal relationships, as well as business relations, the cost of fear in corporate America has contributed to the situation we find ourselves in today.

Management's role is to help team members feel comfortable, help them bring accurate data forward and support them in removing roadblocks to accurate data collection. In addition, support them in not sugar-coating the issues, help them feel comfortable enough to tell the truth and then help them correct the problem. Work shoulder to shoulder with your team members to implement the solutions. This will elicit trust in management, trust in management's actions, and with our newly bonded team, we can all support the entire system together.

Additional tools that I described previously in the organic leader's arsenal, which allow them to create and maintain focus on priorities, is the Pareto Chart. The Pareto Principle is the 80/20 rule that helps you manage those things that really make a difference to results and continuous improvement. Again, this is a proven mathematical formula. Applied to business operations, it shows that only 20 percent of the work (the first 10 percent and the last 10 percent) will remove the errors which are causing the biggest problems, while 80 percent of the problems consume the organization's time and resources.

The 80/20 rule can be applied to practically anything from projects, to capital spending, to root cause analysis, to management's decisions, and can be applied to problems to determine if capital is being spent to eliminate root causes of problems. The value of the Pareto Principle for an organization is that it is a reminder for the organic leader and their team to focus on the 20 percent that matters. Remember, of all the things you focus on and respond to during your day, only 20 percent of them really matter. Twenty percent produces 80 percent of your organization's problems or opportunities! When you identify and focus on the 20 percent, you reduce stress and anxiety. A stress-free environment allows people in the organization to be more productive.

People can get their arms around and understand what to focus on if the problems are smaller rather than larger. Folks not having to respond with constant knee-jerk reactions are happier and more productive. These situations drain everyone's energy and brain power.

Typically in corporate America, team members are not given enough time to do effective root cause analysis. In addition, human capital and money are in short supply to solve problems. Often, when teams make suggestions or recommendations to management on how the problem or opportunity might be removed or improved, thorough root cause analysis has never been performed.

It is the responsibility of the organic leader to ensure that problem focus is kept in the valuable 20 percent.

In studying the execution of strategic plans, capital plans and forecasts in corporate America, what I found is poor scores for management actions. If corporate America was performing stellar, we would not be seeing the issues we are seeing in our economy right now.

I invite you to look underneath what is actually happening in our corporations: poor root cause analysis, lack of training and utilization of systematic tools for improvement.

If CEOs, Boards, and HR executives want to do something to help build America back into a world economic power, they would be well advised to support the systematic use by business of this strategic toolbox: Cause and effect problem solving, Pareto Analysis and long-term strategies which replace short-term quarterly financial firefighting.

There will always be emergencies, but it is not in the best interest of the organization, the employees, the customers or the community to remain in a firefighting mode. For all leaders and managers, the tools discussed previously should serve as a daily reminder to focus 80 percent of their time and energy on 20 percent of the work. But remember this: Make sure the 20 percent you focus on is the RIGHT 20!

The often quoted phrase is to work harder not smarter, but don't just "work smart," work smart on the right things.[25]

---

[25] F. John Reh. Pareto's Principle—The 80/20 Rule. How the 80/20 rule can help you be more effective. http://management.about.com/cs/generalmanagement/a/Pareto081202.html.

Inductive reasoning, cause and effect analysis and the Pareto Principle are the most cost-effective tools ever invented to help your organization grow. In my opinion, no competitor can keep up with a company who is continuously improving, meeting ever-expanding customer expectations and reducing costs.

Dr. Deming used to tell me, "Paula, a company can capture any market in the world with the highest possible quality and the lowest possible cost."

By using these tools, American business could return to greatness. If we could partner with the world, rather than competing with the world for ideas and resources, I believe we could overt a complete collapse of the American economy.

I have no desire to be right. There is too much at stake to worry about the ego and its need to be right. I believe in people, in process and in continuous improvement ... I believe it's the only way out.

CHAPTER TEN

THE SUM OF
THE PARTS

In Western business, the standard management approach is top-down. This is a power-based approach. Because policies and practices are imposed on organizations and people, their natural response is resistance. Therefore, most top-down methods are destined to fail. At the Bama Companies, we recognize that frontline, personalized recommendations and input are more effective and endure over time. This is not a linear approach. The antithesis to top-down is not bottom-up; rather, it is circular, continuous and whole.

While Western culture would like for us to believe that bigger is better, there is no scientific or spiritual evidence that makes that declaration true. As recent events have shown us, there are no economies of scale relative to size. Those who control power and wealth are too often disinterested in solving real problems, and merely consumed with further increasing their power and wealth. Every organization will benefit when they learn to rely on dedicated commitment rather than passive compliance, on consensus rather than coercion, on influence that results from competence rather than hierarchy.

Throughout history, innovation and problem solving have come from individuals whose purpose was not to make money, but to solve problems and make things better for their families and communities. This does not preclude commercialization. Business should prosper and commerce should prevail, but not to the exclusion or belittlement of others.

Instead of managers and leaders obsessively focusing on how to maintain power,, as business leaders we should be questioning why frontline employees' ideas and innovations never make it into the business process or the marketplace. As organic leaders we must ensure that those with good ideas are not disenfranchised and that resources are available to them for experimentation and implementation. It is true that success breeds success. When a company encourages and develops total organizational improvement, the overall business is rewarded by the market as customers realize the benefits of innovation. After all, a company is really just a group of people who interact for a common purpose. They are the ones who make up the organization.[26]

---

[26] Dennis Harting. Employees, Your Most Valuable Asset, Ezine Articles, 15 Dec 2008 <http://ezinearticles.com/?Employees—-Your-Most-Valuable-Asset&id=975567>.

The brain is designed to problem solve and innovate. All technological advancement from the first carved tools to the current hand-held devices is a result of this innate desire and ability. At any given time, an organization is privy to an astonishing number of good ideas. Every organization has the opportunity to encourage and listen and take responsibility. Too often, management concerns itself with blame and finger-pointing rather than problem solving. For an organization to succeed, this blame game must stop. It's about setting priorities, encouraging collaboration, remaining focused on those priorities and being respectful to one another.

At the Bama Companies we came to understand that we needed to let go of blame and talk to each other about what matters and what can and should be fixed. Then we made the commitment to empower everyone in the organization to enact those changes. When people are empowered, they are able to overcome feelings of malaise and helplessness. Their lives are filled with purpose and opportunity. In Stephen Covey's words, "Twenty or thirty years ago, only 30 percent of the value added to goods and services came from knowledge work. Now it's 80 percent. So if companies hope to survive, they must empower people to think for themselves and draw on their experience and wisdom."[27]

---

[27] Stephen Covey. *The Eighth Habit: From Effectiveness to Greatness,* Free Press, New York, 2004.

This means CEOs and managers must develop and sustain a sense of trust in their employees. As Patti Hathaway (a.k.a. The Change Agent) explains, businesses should make a distinction between managers and leaders. Leaders inspire people by encouraging a sense of ownership and accountability among everyone in the organization.[28]

Trust is not a business policy; it must be sincere. The best way to exhibit trust is to ask questions rather than dictate policy. When you ask questions, you must sincerely want to know what the respondent has to say. Effective questions with regards to problem solving and continuous improvement are, "What do you think should be done?" and when ideas are offered, "What do we need to consider in order to implement what you are suggesting?" This encourages people to think about the entire process and optional plans. This instills pride. "The possibility of pride of workmanship means more to the production worker than gymnasiums, tennis courts and recreation areas."[29]

Leaders also understand the importance of silence. Not every idea or recommendation requires an immediate response. People need to be acknowledged and their contributions appreciated, but time should be given to consider all ideas and ample time to evaluate efficacy. Decisions need to be explained

---

[28] Patti Hathaway. www.thechangeagent.com.

[29] W. Edward Deming. *Out of the Crisis*, Massachusetts Institute of Technology, 1982, 78.

in a way that continues to encourage input, even when an idea is not implemented.

Cross training gives people within an organization the opportunity to understand and appreciate other people's roles in an organization. It also helps them discover their own interests and passions. As Covey has observed, "With passion, people don't need supervision; they'll generate creative solutions to problems on their own."[30] This doesn't mean they are renegades; rather, they know the organization is committed to them and in return they are committed to the well-being of the organization. At the Bama Companies, all of our employees know:

1. What their responsibilities are to the organization.

2. What knowledge and training they need to fulfill their responsibilities.

3. How much empowerment they have to respond to situations.

4. When expectations are clear, problems can be solved and processes can be improved.

All intentions are null and void if people within the organization do not have the resources they need to be successful. These resources include tools, training, information and

---

[30] Stephen Covey. *The Eighth Habit: From Effectiveness to Greatness.* Free Press, New York, 2004, 240.

coworkers. Sometimes just knowing who else in the organization has access to particular information or the role of another department can put an employee on the path to problem solving. Providing mentors to new employees and interest groups within the organization lets employees know they are supported. These groups may be made up of people who share expertise, i. e., Accounting, Operations, Six Sigma, People Systems, Supply Chain Systems or Engineering or professional societies. Societies may extend to people beyond the organization who "update" each other on new discoveries and ideas. Discoveries in science, engineering and medicine are important topics to share new news. Human beings love to be part of groups who share like minds. The trust organizations share with their employees means being able to reach beyond the confines of their organizations to the world at large.

Managers often avail themselves of this knowledge, but they need to give their employees the same access. Studies, conferences, meetings and other information-based sharing increase knowledge and stimulate creative thinking. Employees need to have access to the same global innovations and standards as managers and CEOs so they are able to make informed decisions.

Dr. Deming recognized the importance of employee participation in his groundbreaking book *Out of the Crisis* in which he encouraged American companies to follow the Japanese practice of having frontline employees participate in operations, planning and goal setting. Employees should be encouraged to make suggestions and take a relatively high degree of responsibility for overall performance.[31]

If empowerment has not been part of the organization's culture, employees may need training to understand their new responsibilities. This training should include:

1. Determining how the individual can make a contribution to the organization. Show them how contributing can be fulfilling not only at work, but in all areas of their lives.

2. Teaching the individual to take accountability for their own actions while holding others accountable for theirs in the spirit of cooperation.

3. Teaching the individual how to master their own energy. Positive energy produces positive energy. Even problems can be addressed with a positive outlook.

4. Determining individual strengths, qualities and passions. Show them how using their strengths in the service of others leads to happiness within and beyond the organization.

5. Taking pride and ownership in their work by moving beyond "if only" thinking. Their contributions do matter and are attainable.

---

[31] W. Edward Deming. *Out of the Crisis*, Massachusetts Institute of Technology, 1982, 47.

Organizations do require operating guidelines so that everyone knows what is expected, but they should be brief, direct and necessary. What people expect most from an organization and its leaders is parity and honesty. Rather than a complex Human Resource Manual with unenforceable and erratic rules, at the Bama Companies, we have the following guidelines regarding all of our employees:

1. Employees understand they are valued and appreciated.

2. Salaries, benefits, perks and a comfortable work environment are important, but truth, respect and understanding are just as important.

3. Loyalty, honesty and commitment are a two-way process (top-down and bottom-up).

4. Expectations are fully explained and reinforced.

5. Only rules that are necessary and can be enforced are applied.

The organic leader's role is to ensure the organization is comprised of happy, loyal employees who want what is best for each other, their suppliers, customers, community and the planet. This will allow your organization not only to run more smoothly but also provide everyone with more joy and satisfaction.

We all have a commitment to everyone's success. We should all be proactive to ensure that everyone in the organization is able to demonstrate their talents and potential for growth.

CONCLUSION

It seems we are faced with daunting challenges as we enter the second decade of the twenty-first century: corporate scandals, an economy steeped in recession and unending corporate bailouts. We are beset by these problems because we allowed ourselves to operate our businesses and organizations from a place of fear. Fear will not lead us out of the troubled times. Instead, we must be committed to cultivate and grow successful businesses and organizations based upon honesty, integrity and positive energy.

Those at the helm of businesses and organizations must put their egos aside and commit themselves to becoming organic leaders. Each of us must express commitment to our employees, customers, suppliers and communities. We forge this commitment by asking ourselves:

1. Do your employees and customers believe through your words and actions that you are committed to their needs and expectations?

2. Do your employees and customers believe that interacting with your corporations will allow them to be more successful?

3. Do you understand how your products and services meet your customers' and community's needs better than anyone else?

4. Are you utilizing the talents and interests of your staff and employees?

5. Is everyone in your organization treated with respect?

6. How do you measure your commitment?

If we are to regain the corporate prominence of the past, we must commit ourselves to working for the betterment of others instead of ourselves. When CEOs and managers in their organizations are focused on keeping their positions and prominence instead of improving the lives of others, their organizations are already in decline. Those who care only about maintaining their position, income and perceived importance have no interest in creating value or purpose for others; without value or purpose, there is no reason for your organization to exist.

Our employees, customers, suppliers and consumers all respond to purpose and worth. An organic leader recognizes this universal truth and remains committed to helping people channel their skills, expand their abilities and generate positive energy into their shared environment. Every encounter we have with another human being is an opportunity to inspire. From inspiration comes knowledge, growth and continuous improvement.

Dr. Deming said it the best. "Long-term commitment to new learning and new philosophy is required of any management that seeks transformation. The timid and fainthearted and people who expect quick results are doomed to disappointment."[32] What Deming had to teach us about business is as relevant today as it was a half-century ago. "The job of management is inseparable from the welfare of the company."[33] Through our commitment to the well-being of others, we can revive not only our businesses and our economy, but also our world.

I am a privileged soul. I am the CEO of our family's business and have been honored to work with some of the greatest people in our world today. I am grateful for everything I have learned from them and hope in sharing their lessons with you, you will take the opportunity to inspire and improve your own organizations. Our businesses and organizations can be more than mere instruments of commerce; they can be places that celebrate humanity and honor our souls.

Both the marketplace and universe will respond to this positive energy by rewarding all people committed to the common cause of purpose, respect and continuous improvement.

---

[32] Ibid., x.

[33] Ibid.

My family, friends and teammates are the lights of my life. Please enjoy some of the photos I have taken on my journey through life. I love them all, and we are all united in the common causes of life's purpose, respect and continuous improvement!

Together in life, we can do ANYTHING!!!!

Mom and her grandson and her great grandkids ...
she's my partner in business and life!!

Spending time understanding nature.

My kids and grandkids are the loves and lights of my life.

These are the loves of my life, my daughter and granddaughter!!

My other granddaughter is on the left!!
Her mom is on the left above.

My boys are the best!!!

My friends bring me great joy and common purposes.

My adopted kids are lights in a sometimes dark world.

My adopted godparents!! Doc and Polly …
He knows more about medicine than anyone!!

And finally, me and my angels ... celebration time....

MINE IS A BLESSED LIFE ... THANKS BE TO GOD....

I hope you enjoy the book, and if you manage people, or lead a group or a company ... please make your organization better and better every day. That is needed and is expected.

Sincerely,

Paula

RECOMMENDED RESOURCES

Associates in Process Improvement. Lloyd Provost and Tom Nolan, http://www.apiweb.org/associates.html.

Bartlett, John. *Bartlett's Familiar Quotations,* Sixteenth edition, Little Brown and Co.,1992.

Bobinski, Dan and Dennis Rader. *Living Toad Free: Overcoming Resistance to Motivation,* Xulon Press, 2004.

Buckingham, Marcus and Donald O. Clifton. *First Break All the Rules, Now: Discover Your Strengths,* Free Press, 2001.

_____. *Go: Put Your Strengths to Work,* Free Press, 2007.

Dusty Staub, *Courage of the Heart, Heart Led Leadership,* Council Oak Press, 2001.

Chanski, Christopher. *Principled Performance: From the Mailroom to the Boardroom,* River City Press, Inc., 2007.

Charan, Ram. *What the CEO Wants You to Know,* Crown Press, New York, 2001.

Cohen, Philip. Deming's 14 Points, http://www.hci.com.au/hcisite2/articles/deming.html, 12/21/08.

Covey, Stephen R. *The Eighth Habit: From Effectiveness to Greatness,* Free Press, New York, 2004.

_____. and A. Roger Merrell. *First Things First,* Free Press, 1996.

_____. *The Seven Habits of Highly Effective People,* Fifteenth edition, Free Press, 2004.

Deming, William Edward. *The New Economics for Industry, Government, Education,* Second edition, Massachusetts Institute of Technology Press, 2000.

_____. *Out of the Crisis,* Massachusetts Institute of Technology Press, 1982.

_____. *Some Theory of Sampling,* Dover Publications, 1984, www.deming.org.

Drucker, Peter. www.drukerinstitute.com.

Gardner, John W. *On Leadership,* Free Press, 1993.

Gladwell, Malcolm. Blink: *The Power of Thinking without Thinking,* Back Bay Books, 2007.

Govier, Trudy. *Practical Study of Argument,* Wadsworth Publishing, Sixth edition, 2004.

Harting, Dennis. "Employees, Your Most Valuable Asset," Ezine Articles, 15 Dec 2008. <http://ezinearticles.com/?Employees---Your-Most-Valuable-Asset&id=975567.

Hathaway, Patti. www.thechangeagent.com.

Hrebiniak, Lawrence. *Making Strategy Work: Adding Effective Execution and Change,* Wharton School Publishing, 2005.

Junious, Ellen Denise. *Unleash the Power of Personal Advantage: 7 Keys to Unlock Your Potential for Success,* iUniverse, Inc., 2007.

Losoncy, Lewis. *The Motivating Team Leader,* DC Press, Sanford, Florida, 2003.

Marshall, Paul. *A Piece of the Pie,* Walsworth Press, Inc., 1987.

www.Morebusiness.com.

Myss, Carolyn. Sacred Contracts, www.myss.com/CMED/media/.

_____ . *Anatomy of the Spirit, The Seven Stages of Power and Healing.*

Rhodes, Lewis A. "The Profound Knowledge School," http://www.newhorizons.org/trans/rhodes.htm. 12/21/08 lewrhodes@aol.com.

Purkey, William. *Psycho-Cybernetics: Self-Concept and School Achievement,* Prentice Hall, 1960.

Reh, John F. *Pareto's Principle—The 80/20 Rule. How the 80/20 rule can help you be more effective.* ttp://management.about.com/cs/generalmanagement/a/Pareto081202.html.

Seligman, Martin. *Learned Optimism: How to Change Your Mind and Your Life,* Simon and Schuster, Inc., New York, 1990.

Smith, Alicia. "The Business Ego Trap: Having an Ego in Business," www.morebuiness.com, June 5, 2006.

Vance, Mike and Diane Deacon. *Break Out of the Box*, Career Press, New Jersey, 1996.

Wallace, Ken. "8 Ways to Listen for True Understanding." Franklin Covey, online. http://www.teambuildingtips.com/team-building-articles/team-communication/8-ways-to-listen-for-true-understanding.html.

Wren, J. Thomas. *The Leader's Companion: Insights on Leadership Through the Ages*, Free Press, 1995.